Praise fo

PR used to be an egotistical exercise in pitching the media based on your (or your clients') agenda. In an always-on world, the best approach to generating media attention and to reaching buyers directly is to create content they love to consume and are eager to share. Lisa Buyer shows you how.

**David Meerman Scott, bestselling author of *The New Rules of Marketing and PR*, now in over 25 languages from Bulgarian to Vietnamese.
@dmscott**

Effective public relations execution continues to evolve, especially in the high-tech software industry. Social PR Secrets, is packed full of actionable, real-world tactics that we put to use in our company with immediate results. My team found the numerous nuggets of information in the book to be easy to read and act upon. It's a must-read for your PR or marketing team.

**Ron Antevy, President and CEO e-Builder, Inc. an SaaS company
@ebuilder**

With Social PR Secrets, Buyer has delivered a well-researched and insightful exploration of the latest social media and PR principles and techniques in a practical and enjoyable book that pushes the boundaries of the art and science of optimizing and socializing your business' news. A definite must-read that ought to be required reading for anyone serious about social media.

**Brett Tabke, founder and CEO of Pubcon, the premier optimization and new media conferences
@pubcon**

Leading the way from traditional to Social PR, Lisa's expertise and proven methods empower PR and marketing professionals to successfully leverage today's social, digital landscape to promote the brand. A must-have reference!

Rebecca Murtagh, CEO, speaker, and author of Million Dollar Websites: Build a Better Website Using Best Practices of the Web Elite @virtualmarketer

@lisabuyer is a scary little mash up of what it's actually like to actually implement hybrid digital PR. Of all the thought leaders we've interacted with, Lisa's one of the few that totally walks the walk. She thinks about PR from the perspective of social psychographic distribution by organic and paid channels for the win. Social PR Secrets is an easy-to-consume handbook laced with tasty ideas and techniques useful for PR professionals at any level.

Marty Weintraub, author of *The Complete Social Media Community Manger's Guide*, Founder and Evangelist @aimClear

Extremely informative and designed for those marketing professionals who, like me, have a short attention span. Social PR Secrets, is a must read! The online public relations industry continues to evolve as fast—if not faster—than the digital space itself. Whether you are representing yourself or your clients online, Lisa is the perfect guide when it comes to informative tips and strategies on delivering company news outside the traditional journalism ecosystem across social media, mobile devices, and visual press releases—all of which must be optimized for search engines.

Matt McGowan, Managing Director, Incisive Media @matt_mcgowan

Want to impress your client? Buy this book. A quick, practical guide by a PR veteran on crafting campaigns that perform.

Dennis Yu, Chief Executive Officer, BlitzMetrics
@dennisyu

An action oriented book by a PR wizard, Lisa delivers. Buy this book if you're looking for ideas you can use immediately to drive press for your clients.

Nathan Latka, CEO and Co-Founder of Heyo
@nathanlatka

Search Engine Optimization, influence marketing, and PR are all converging and part the mix now; perfect timing for Social PR Secrets. Social in Public Relations needs to go from being a task assigned to the intern or newest employee fresh out of college—and central to the whole agency. No PR professional can afford to be without this knowledge.

Ric Dragon, author of *Social Marketology* and CEO of DragonSearch
@ricdragon

Lisa Buyer painstakingly practices what she preaches. She's a doer, an experimenter, and is constantly learning so she can remain the PR trendmaster that she is. Her dedication to online servant leadership, freely offering so much of her knowledge, is what you get in real life too. She's a true example of the modern day PR professional—a digital nomad with the ability to think like a producer and editor and be the consummate brand advocate.

Sarah Evans, Digital Correspondent and author of
[Re]frame: Little Inspirations for a Larger Purpose
@prsarahevans

SOCIAL
PR
SECRETS

How to Optimize, Socialize,
and Publicize Your Brand

LISA BUYER

Hashtag: #SocialPRSecrets

**Social PR Secrets doesn't stop here. Join the conversation by
following the hashtag #SocialPRSecrets, or check out these
websites for updates of Lisa Buyer's PR Secrets publications
and events:** lisabuyer.com.

Published by JETLAUNCH (www.jetlaunch.net)

Lisa Buyer photo credit Emily Banks, Anna Maria Island, Florida

Illustrations by Lauren Donovan

facebook.com/deepcereal

@beebow (www.twitter.com/beebow)

Dedication

There have been many lives and many masters in my life. This book is dedicated to my dad, he always wanted to write a book about his memoirs, and to Tracy, she never dreamed her life would be cut short and there would be a book about her death.

To my mom, she proofed this book and my life.

Contents

Foreword

If PR people don't embrace social media, they will be left in the dust. The concept of sucking up to a few major publications and offering exclusives to the one that promises the most coverage is a risky concept.

For one thing, the major publications no longer "make" products and services; they often report on products and services that have been made. Trickle down is waning. Bubble up is the new game.

Thus, PR and social media are completely different. Where PR is about getting journalists to tell people to buy your product. Social media is about providing value. The goals, rules, and best-practices are not the same.

We are fortunate that Lisa has written this book to help PR people understand this brave, new world. She provides tactical and practical methods to combine the best of both worlds. We're lucky that she has done this for marketers, PR people, and entrepreneurs.

Guy Kawasaki
Chief evangelist of Canva
and former chief evangelist of Apple

Acknowledgments

Writing the third edition of *Social PR Secrets* is an honor! Working in the social media and PR business is life in the fast lane with changes happening on a daily basis. New networks, apps and algorithms change more often than not. That's why this third edition was a must with eight new chapters and a refresh on the entire book.

Two years after publishing the original *Social PR Secrets*, I'm teaching Social Media Management at the University of Florida College of Journalism and I love my class @UFSMM. Thank you @UFJschool's Professor John Wright for making it all possible and Juan-Carlos Molleda for believing in me.

Special thanks to the publishing pros who played a major role in getting this next book from point A to B to P (for published) Chris O'Byrne, president of JETLAUNCH (www.jetlaunch.net) and his dynamic team.

Pinning to the top of my daily feed: Social PR do-er Navah Berg helps keep me focused and mindful on a daily basis. Newcomers to my circles of faves include Nick Cicero and Cathy Hackl. Hugs to Daniela Iozano who helped in the proofing process. High five to my business coach @CharlieGilkey for my playbook.

I had a ton of collective advice from authors who shared their book-writing tips and publishing war stories with me. Huggable thanks to Guy Kawasaki, David Meerman Scott, Marty Weintraub, Greg Jarboe, Mel Carson, Ric Dragon, Krista Neher, Rebecca Murtagh, and those authors that I follow for inspiration and style. Inspiration gratitude to Gretchen Rubin, Tony Robbins, Tony Hsieh, and Elizabeth Gilbert.

The business and life mentors that have helped shape me over the years: Dan Chiodo, Uncle Carl, and Paige Rose.

Thanks to the love (and partner) of my life Don, for always believing in me and supporting me.

I would not have loved writing this book and looking at it every day on my bookshelf if it wasn't for Lauren Donovan aka @deepcereal. It was Lauren who illustrated the chapter intros and makes the whole book come to life.

Introduction

by Sarah Evans, Digital Correspondent and author of *[Re]frame: Little Inspirations for a Larger Purpose*

Lisa Buyer painstakingly practices what she preaches. She's a doer, an experimenter, and is constantly learning so she can remain the PR trendmaster that she is. Her dedication to online servant leadership, freely offering so much of her knowledge, is what you get in real life too. She's a true example of the modern day PR professional—a digital nomad with the ability to think like a producer and editor and be the consummate brand advocate.

Whether it's media relations, social strategy, or internal communications, companies are looking for more efficient and effective ways to use emerging and established technologies.

If you work in a slow-moving, behemoth of a company, small victories—like establishing a Facebook page—are the result of months, if not years, of campaigning. For those who are in smaller or more agile companies, you may be the frontrunners, jumping on new technologies as they become available. Either way, you're likely tasked with staying in the know and monitoring all things social.

Consider *Social PR Secrets* the communication professional's modern-day beginner's handbook. It may appear to have a light-hearted or whimsical approach, but therein lies its brilliance. The non-threatening format allows anyone to feel comfortable reading while they are exposed to tactical and practical public relations tips.

Trying to learn all the nuances and theories of search and optimization, social and publicity takes years of work, and that doesn't include all of the trial and error during stages of tactical application. And because things change quickly, what you learn could change in an instant. It requires daily diligence to stay on top of your craft.

Lisa thoughtfully lays out some of the more common roles the PR person of today plays, from the editorial to managing online communities to reporting results. At the very least, the book provides you with a realistic view of the communications landscape and at the most, shares some of the most valuable information you can use. Right. Now.

I challenge you to make *Social PR Secrets* a personalized guide for how you work. Treat it as your baseline, ready to help you grow faster than you could without it. Make notes in the margins, challenge what you read, or better yet, share your experiences with others (#SocialPRSecrets).

It's an exciting time to work in the communications industry. We are in a time of constant change, but some things will always remain the same. We exist to connect a brand with their stakeholders, keep consumers coming back, and to share stories.

@prsarahevans
Digital Correspondent

Chapter 1
Social PR Evolution and Revolution

Social PR Evolution

Have You Tried Google?

'll never forget the day, it was in the year 2000, that one of my employees popped into my office with the question, "Have you tried Google?" At the time, my PR agency was already immersed in all things digital, working in the go-go dot-com days, and we were curious to learn.

My traditional PR background meant a heavy focus on generating print and broadcast media coverage for emerging technology clients. Before the digital days, everything revolved around print press releases, media tours, and trade shows. The journalist was the gatekeeper and the key—and still is, in many ways—to generating publicity through their coverage of a story. Working with dot-com technology start-ups in the boom, the generation of editorial coverage meant the difference between a company impressing the investment community enough to get funded or going under in obscurity.

PR campaigns for dot-com start-ups moved at a fast and furious clip. What had once taken months to plan and execute was now reduced to weeks or even days. News began to surface faster, thanks to search engines like Yahoo! and Google. We discovered tricks in press release distribution that helped us not only reach journalists in a more direct way, but also deliver news directly to certain online segments and groups.

The early days of optimization meant adding a stock symbol to an online press release to automatically land it in the email inbox of investors tracking that company. Similarly, using links in a digital press release would assist in search visibility and the delivery of traffic to that website. For example, in the ticker symbol example, you might see how this compares to the way hashtags are used today in social media news messaging and how we can target the "likes" and "interests" of Facebook users. The most basic digital targeting and efficiencies helped us understand the opportunity in those early days.

As search engines evolved (and Google became a household name), marketers raced to figure out ways to climb to the top of search results. Meanwhile, the Dot-com bubble bombed and September 11, 2001 tragedies happened, sending the entire business community into a state of shock. PR professionals began to be perceived as a luxury to businesses who were asking, "What is the ROI?" "How could you prove it?" "What were organizations actually getting from all this editorial coverage?" and "Was it all just fluff?"

In reality, traditional PR is hard to measure and justify. Thanks to the Internet, digital public relations became the clear winner in terms of leveling the playing field and creating opportunities for small and large brands. The key to successful PR now lies in understanding how to balance the optimization of news content for search engines, social media, and human readers. Google News began serving up company press releases some time ago, and systems such as Google Alerts allow us to monitor industry news, competitor mentions, and our own brand mentions.

Marketers flocked to this new opportunity. The PR industry had a rebirth to garner incredible results for clients through a working knowledge of the basic practices of search engine marketing and optimization. Editorial coverage from various online news sources ranked in Google meant public relations had a new set of key performance indicators (KPIs): online visibility, ranking in search engine results, and the influence and referral of quality visitors to a website.

Ever Heard of Facebook?

Sarah Van Elzen asked me, "Have you heard of Facebook?" in January of 2007 after her graduation from the University of Minnesota. She was in her first week as an interactive PR coordinator. Active on Facebook as a student, Sarah gave me the social heads up—that is, to "ditch MySpace and check out Facebook."

After a little experimenting, I discovered Facebook was not just a social network for college kids. It had the potential to become a massive PR media outlet, giving brands a way to socialize the news message, share news, and influence publicity through online coverage—and it certainly has. By late 2007, Facebook had more than 100,000 business pages. It soon became a key component in the social PR process to set up a new client with a Facebook Business Page, YouTube channel, and relative social media profiles. In addition to gaining publicity within the social networks, applying search engine optimization (SEO) best practices to social media profiles carried the added bonus of helping companies secure positive branded search results.

Are You on Twitter?

This was the big question at Pubcon in 2007, where I was really geeking my way out of the traditional public relations world and entering a new solar system with planets such as Google, Facebook, and Twitter. I joined Twitter right before the conference and began following news about the speakers and sessions. The keyword here is "news," as Twitter had quickly become yet another opportunity for PR pros to report and share news digitally and in real time. Engagement and interaction were huge factors, even in those early days. Tweeting became an essential part of the social PR arsenal.

PR Put a Man on The Moon, What Can it Do For You?

Content marketing is all the rage today, but did you know the greatest content marketing case in human history actually occurred in the late 1960s and early 1970s?

It began when President John F. Kennedy stood before Congress in 1961 and made it a goal to put a man on the moon before the decade was over. The end result was the historic landing of Apollo 11.

"It's actually the greatest story never told (until now) about content as a marketing and public relations tool that helped to deliver humans to the moon," said David Meerman Scott, most notable for writing *The New Rules of Marketing and PR* and coining the term "newsjacking." In 2014, he released: *Marketing the Moon: The Selling of the Apollo Lunar Program*.

Marketing Space for the United States

A departure from his usual social media and digital flight pattern, Scott's *Marketing the Moon* tells the story of how NASA not only put the first man on the moon, but pioneered the use of brand journalism, product placement, and real-time storytelling with the epitome of transparency and authenticity.

For the space enthusiasts and sci-fi cult-followers who create and follow the GIFs and memes branded with *Star Wars*, *Space Odyssey*, and *Star Trek*, *Marketing the Moon* captures the challenges and the ultimate success of marketing one of the greatest achievements in American history as noted in the foreword written by Captain Eugene A. Cernan, the NASA astronaut who became the 11th person to walk on the Moon (en.wikipedia.org/wiki/List_of_people_who_have_walked_on_the_Moon)   and "the last man on the Moon."

Scott wrote *Marketing the Moon* with Richard Jurek, president of Inland Marketing & Communications. They share the lifelong passion of being enthusiasts and collectors of historic space artifacts from the Apollo program. It was that passion and collective dedication that allowed them to take this opportunity to curate the historical data in a time capsule-like book filled with nostalgic marketing memorabilia.

"It's been a blast to dig into marketing history by speaking with half the men who walked on the moon, NASA public affairs staff, the PR people from contractors like Boeing and Raytheon, and journalists from publications like *The New York Post* and *Reuters* – part of the hundreds and thousands of unsung participants from the golden age of spaceflight," Scott said.

8 Social PR Lessons from *Marketing the Moon*

What once was old, now is new and improved. Content marketing is nothing new, but its recent popularity surge has marketers scrambling to get it right or crash and burn.

"Many marketers are over the moon about the *new* concept of content marketing as a key component to SEO; few realize that content marketing has been around for 50 years in an offline world," said Scott. "Fundamentals are important, so looking back informs us how to go forward. While everybody is looking for the next big thing, I found inspiration by going back half a century," Scott said.

1. **Teach your PR and content marketing department to work as reporters, act like journalists.** This is NASA's content marketing approach to PR. In practice, Public Information Office staff worked as reporters within the agency, seeking out newsworthy information from NASA technical personnel and processing it into a form useful to the press.

2. **Hire former journalists who are good writers and understand the news business.** Walter T. Bonney, the head of NASA's nascent Public Information Office made it his business that NASA's public affairs group did not act as pitchmen, but as reporters. Bonney, a former journalist, actively sought and recruited staff with print and broadcast media experience. Among those Bonney enlisted during the early days of the agency were Paul

Haney and Jack King, who would soon play key roles during the Apollo program. "The core contingent of NASA Public Affairs people—just about all of us—were ex-newsmen," King told Scott in a lengthy interview. "We were good writers, and we knew the news business. That made a major difference in the whole operation."

3. **Create materials and content that address the needs of your audience.** The NASA Public Affairs Office's growing ranks of journalists understood what constituted a good story and what details appealed to the press. Thus, NASA created materials that addressed reporters' needs in press releases, bylined articles, background materials, sponsored media symposiums, television newsreels, and fully produced radio broadcasts complete with interviews and sound effects. This content output helped to feed a world hungry for information about America's space efforts, and leave the world's press outlets receptive and clamoring for content to serve up to their audiences.

4. **Awesome content lasts forever and is what creates history.** "Content was not only king during Apollo, it was also one of the earliest successful brand journalism campaigns in history," Scott said.

5. **Learning as you go pays off; with risk comes great rewards.** "Don't think for a moment that NASA masterminded a PR campaign that brought the Apollo missions into our living rooms. Just like everything else about the Moon program, how and how much to share Apollo with the public was a learn-as-you-go affair that involved not only NASA's Public Affairs Office but also top NASA managers and even astronauts," said Andrew Chaikin, author of *A Man on the Moon* in his review of *Marketing the Moon*.

6. **Transparency and authenticity still wins.** Even for Neil Armstrong, the first man to step onto the surface of the

moon, NASA did not script his famous words or give him any direction on what to say. During arguably one of the most-watched global television events in history, NASA gave him the personal freedom, as they did for all the other astronauts, to make his own statements and speak his own mind.

7. **Brand journalism orbits content marketing yesterday and today.** NASA didn't have a massive PR machine that worked to shape the global press image of the astronauts and the program. Staffed largely by professional journalists, the NASA Public Affairs Office operated more like a newsroom to rapidly disseminate information to the world press. More than 3,000 reporters covered the Apollo 11 mission from the Cape and Houston, while many thousands around the world worked from home.

8. **Reporting versus selling.** "NASA was not "spinning" or "selling" the space program, but reporting it in a remarkably open way in as close to real-time as the technology of the time allowed," said Scott.

Social PR Revolution

What does Google have to do with PR?

My first search marketing conference was Search Engine Strategies (now called ClickZ) in December 2006. I remember calling a friend right after Danny Sullivan's "Intro to Search Marketing" session feeling like I had just received my MBA. The opportunity for PR to not only capitalize on search, but to actually influence it, opened my eyes to a new world of digital PR possibilities.

Everything in search at that time was about content—and still is. When you think about it, everything in public relations is about content, whether via a press release, media story, blog post, image, social media message, or executive bio. The success of any given campaign largely depends on the efficacy of content in attracting attention and influencing a particular outcome. I became addicted to learning this new way of marketing and understanding how I could apply it to my public relations practice, ideally helping clients translate this into their own business success.

A complete newbie to the online marketing scene, it was in 2007 that I found ways to educate myself in Internet marketing best practices. It was horrifying to find out that the new website I had just launched was not SEO-friendly, although beautifully built in Flash. Ugh! It was hard for me to give my business card out until I had changed my website to HTML and started a blog. Not only did I believe this would be the new way of doing PR, but I also wanted to differentiate my agency in our PR service offerings. I immediately connected with online PR pros Lee Odden and Greg Jarboe, both SES speakers, and still remember attending Dana Todd's "PPC 101" (pay-per-click) session. I felt inspired at how she took the complicated subject of PPC and made it easy to understand the process of setting up Google Ads using keywords. This new world actually helped me learn new ways to make headlines stand out in search and inspire a user to click through to a full story. I decided to get my Google AdWords certification for the value it would have to my PR career, but also to fine-tune my search engine knowledge.

Blogging for PR

Discovering how easy it was to start a blog using platforms like Blogger or WordPress, coupled with my new SEO knowledge, meant blogs became a staple in my public relations weapon arsenal. In 2007, a PR and marketing audit for an IT client led to a recommendation that they should start a blog as a means to educate the industry as a thought leader. The CEO thought it was brilliant, yet senior management could not get their heads around why they would give out free information to the public. Thankfully, that was then, and attitudes have since changed substantially. More than 60% of companies now have corporate blogs, and most understand the value of thought leadership, authenticity, transparency, and visibility.

Source: onforb.es/1Y0XbNH

"Social Media is All Fun and Games, But We Need to do Real PR"

That email came from a client back in 2008 as we were setting up YouTube channels, Facebook Pages, and social news networks as part of their PR strategy. If that client had only seen the opportunity, the gains as an early social media adopter would have been incredible. Simply having a Facebook Page was once good PR. Getting quality fans and followers was much easier and less expensive because there was little competition. Today, a successful social presence as part of an overarching PR strategy is deeper and more comprehensive. The opportunities are greater than ever, but so is the competition.

Telling an Influential Blogger to F*** Off

Six months into joining the conversation on Twitter as a Social PR strategist, I received a frantic call from Sarah Van Elzen. As I was driving to my daughter's school to pick her up, Sarah gave me terrible news that one of my employees had just told a blogger to "f*** off" on Twitter. That blogger had, in turn, posted a story about The Buyer Group's PR tactics and also called out one of my clients.

If you searched our company name on Google, the story was on the first page of search results within 24 hours. I immediately contacted the blogger and apologized for my employee's online behavior and poor choice of actions. I then assured her it was not part of our agency's best practices to act like that in person, let alone on a social media platform. The blogger went on to write a follow-up story about how impressed she was with how professionally the situation was handled with immediate attention and responsibility for the issue. This new, positive story trumped the negative story on Google. Unbelievably, it all happened within 24 hours.

The lines between social media and PR may at times be blurred, yet they become crystal clear once you realize the potential impact of a single social interaction. Social media has the power to make or break a brand in a snippet of text—or in one compromising photo or scandalous video you thought no one would ever see.

PR Peace, Love, and Social Media

The day an employee told an influential blogger to f*** off was one of the worst days of my professional life. However, here I am, touting social media as a great tool for increasing both search and social visibility. That experience actually turned into a case study for my SES panel presentation when I was invited to speak on how to use Twitter for PR at SES New York the following year. CMOs' jaws dropped and people gasped and cringed when I told the story, yet it was a huge lesson to take back to their organizations. We all learned a valuable lesson on proactive communication and facing potential PR disasters surfacing in social media head-on.

Duluth

Thanks to globetrotting speaker, Marty Weintraub, author of *The Complete Social Media Manager's Guide* and *Killer Facebook Ads: Mastering Cutting-Edge Facebook Advertising Techniques*, and co-founder of the aimClear online marketing agency, I made my fourth trip to Duluth, Minnesota, in 2014 alongside 30 other search and social marketing thought leaders. Marty and I began chatting in the speaker room at a 2010 Pubcon conference and before I knew it, I'd been booked on a flight to aimClear's hometown of Duluth in the middle of January. My task was to work with the aimClear team on putting together content for the now famous aimClear Marketing Workshops @SMX, a full day of educational Facebook content for marketers.

I spent 2011 on the road traveling with the aimClear team to SMX West, SMX Advanced, and SMX East, offering up the latest to marketers looking for insider guidance on the nuances of Facebook. Sitting through those full-day sessions, I realized how Facebook Ads could help amplify the reach of company news content using the Facebook targeting tools to promote posts.

Social PR Secret

Leverage the power of social advertising to promote and amplify reach in the social media newsfeeds. Generate publicity using a blend of organic and paid social PR.

You Say You Want a Revolution

There's so much chatter in the social media and PR worlds. A myriad of people with varying skill sets and areas of expertise have all laid claim to the "social media expert" title, yet what credentials does a social media expert have? Public relations professionals typically have a four-year degree and accreditation. However, PR is a very cluttered and fragmented world with the influx of social media and the continued rising influence of search. It's become more challenging than ever to decipher not only what is important to your brand and which tactics to employ, but how to do it and who to trust to manage it. There's no shortage of books that cover the case studies and theory of it all, and many professionals talk a big talk.

Yet, when it comes time to deliver, the smoke and mirrors come to light. Nobody knows everything. I know I learn something new each day. I could easily focus my business on 100% educational training and forget implementation, but I believe in being exposed on the front lines, and seeing first-hand how technologies and tactics integrate in order to improve the public relations opportunity.

We All Want to Change the World

The paradigm shift in the media world has been dramatic and extreme in its scope. Print is shrinking, digital is expanding, and big data is exploding. The evolution and revolution of PR happens in shorter spurts and higher jumps. Try to visualize the evolution of PR in icons, it would look like a mash of emojis, typewriters, newspapers, televisions, phones, fax machines, email inboxes, chat rooms, Facebook, Snapchat, Instagram, Live Streaming Apps, Twitter, LinkedIn, YouTube, Google, Skype, chat, iPhones, iPads, apps, and infographics. Publicity can change your brand's world in a day—for better or for worse. Landing that *one* story in *The Wall Street Journal*, making the Inc. list, or tweeting out of the wrong account and ending up the trending topic on *Today* are all that much more possible now.

We'd All Love to See the Plan

Talk is cheap, life is short, and PR plans are made to be broken. I've learned a TON from the practical experience of working through big PR failures and small social media mistakes. Having a plan is important, but more critical is an entrepreneur-like mentality and the impetus to move quickly and take action. We need flexibility, especially when it comes to building a PR plan that integrates the unpredictable nature of daily news. In the social PR world, today's news is your news; it's what you make of it and how you embed your brand in it. So, what does the social PR plan look like, and how do we get started?

Spin it Forward

The rest of this book takes you on a practical tour of today's social PR secrets. You'll work your way through an organized set of chapters on inspiring ways you can do it yourself, impress your clients or boss, and optimize the relationship between social and PR. Here we go!

Chapter 2
Today's Media Relations

When Suzanne Somers started researching expert sources for her *New York Times* bestseller, *Ageless: The Naked Truth About Bioidentical Hormones*, she started with a Google search using the keywords "bioidentical hormone therapy doctors." What came to the top page of her Google search was one of the press releases announcing the opening of my client, Dr. Paul Savage's hormone therapy practice in Chicago. What happened next? Dr. Savage landed a phone interview with Suzanne and contributed a full chapter to her book.

So with a little extra effort by paying attention to keywords and optimization, look what is possible:

- An opportunity to be published as a guest author in a celebrity book
- Show up on the first page of a Google search
- Get your story shared in social and media coverage
- Drive quality traffic to your website with your own published content

Welcome to the new media relations! Getting social with PR, and media relations, starts with getting your brand's news optimized with the search engines.

The primary methods of media relations used to be phone, fax, email, mailing, in-person interview, or a trade show conference. Today, all the mixing and mingling happens online via search and social. An even larger shift with media is the new opportunity for each media person to brand themselves individually. Social media news networks can offer a direct line to mainstream media and in many ways can help secure major stories and/or influential coverage.

The Search and Social Media Opportunity

The vast majority of today's journalists use search engines such as Google and social media networks as a research tool to either begin, confirm, or fact-check stories. With that in mind, it's strategic to optimize your news stories with keywords, keyword phrases, tags, shareable content, and links so the media can find you when researching on search and social. Make content that entices the user to click!

Getting Social with the Media

- Identify the social networks for your target media: Where are they hanging out and what are they talking about or interested in?
- Follow them and spark up an online conversation.
- Interact and even collaborate (what a concept!) with the media in social.
- Share their stories.
- Leave comments on their stories and blogs.
- Update all your media lists with the social networks IDs.

Social PR Secret
Create a social media list dashboard using a platform such as Tweetdeck or Hootsuite that enables you to see at a glance the social news stream of what is happening with the media you follow.

Or just create a Twitter list for your media target natively in Twitter. Something like, "Media I love" and make it public so they can see you added them.

Social PR and Media Relation Sources

HARO (www.helpareporter.com) *(Help a Reporter Out)*: Reverse it! Brands can use HARO not just to be in the daily know of journalists looking for story sources, but also to research case studies, produce white papers, and create infographics for them to easily use.

MuckRack (muckrack.com): Social PR pros understand that Twitter is a tool and not a toy. MuckRack is where journalists and sources connect. Find, follow, and send spam-free pitches to journalists you need to know.

Inkybee (www.inkybee.com): for blogger outreach.

BuzzStream (buzzstream.com): Social, PR and SEO management, a web-based platform that helps build authentic relationships with word-of-mouth influencers across the social web.

Talkwalker Alerts (www.talkwalker.com/alerts) Monitor the Web for interesting new content about by adding a search query for the media lists you are targeting.

Anewstip (anewstip.com) Anewstip Search allows you to search for relevant media contacts by things they have written or tweeted.

Radio Guest List (www.radioguestlist.com) This is the HARO of the audio world. You can sign up for email notifications from journalists and podcast hosts who are looking for experts on specific topics.

Twitter Chats

Twitter chats are interactive conversations that happen on Twitter with a group of people all using the same hashtag and a certain topic. To take a deeper dive into the Social PR industry, follow some of these Twitter chats, discover your own, or start one for your industry or brand.

Twitter chats* to make your social PR day:

- **#Sundays**

  #ContentChat (twitter.com/hashtag/ContentChat?src=hash)
  3 p.m. ET

  #BlogChat (twitter.com/search?q=Blogchat)
  9 p.m. ET

- **#Mondays**

  #SocialChat (twitter.com/search?q=SocialChat)
  9 p.m. ET

- **#Tuesdays**

  #GetRealChat (twitter.com/search?q=GetRealChat)
  2 p.m. ET

  #PR20Chat (twitter.com/pr20chat)
  8 p.m. ET

  #LinkedInChat (twitter.com/search?q= LinkedInChat)
  8 p.m. ET

  #InfluencerChat (twitter.com/
  search?q=%23influencerchat&src=typd)
  8 p.m. ET

  #SocialCafe (twitter.com/socialcafechat)
  9 p.m. ET

- **#Wednesdays**

  #BrandChat (twitter.com/search?q=BrandChat)
  11 a.m. ET

  #BufferChat (twitter.com/search?q=BufferChat)
  12 p.m. ET

  #WJChat (twitter.com/search?q=WJchat)
  8 p.m. ET

  #PinChat (twitter.com/search?q=PinChat)
  9 p.m. ET

- **#Thursdays**

  #SEOchat (twitter.com/search?q=SEOchat)
  1 p.m. ET

  #PRProChat (twitter.com/
  search?q=%23PRProchat&src=typd)
  3 p.m. ET (First Thursday of every month)

- **#Fridays**

#BusinessFuel (twitter.com/search?q=BusinessFuel)
1 p.m. ET

- **#Saturdays:**

Take the day off and try a #yoga class!

* Please check your local Twitter listing, programming times subject to change or cancel without a tweet notice.

#Hashtags and Media Relations

A hashtag is a word or phrase prefixed with the symbol #. It's a form of metadata. Short messages on social networking services such as Twitter, Google+, Instagram, Pinterest, and Facebook are indexed when hashtags are used to group messages together.

Hashtracking.com: For your social PR intelligence to get the full story, this is a "go-to" source when looking for event insights, news trends, and meme tracking.

Social Mention (socialmention.com): It works like Google Alerts for social media, hashtags, and more.

Rite Tag (www.ritetag.com): This helps you reach beyond your followers with the right social optimization tags.

#tagboard (tagboard.com): Let's you search any hashtag and create "tagboards." A great way to collect and display social content from events, topics, and branded hashtag posts. It's the new version of the clipping book!

Hashtagify (hashtagify.me) Search and find the best Twitter hashtags to reach your target audience.

Hashatit (www.hashatit.com) An easy way to sort through hashtags, bringing all conversation to one place, real-time.

Twubs (twubs.com) A place to search, register and even brand a specific hashtag.

Keyhole (keyhole.co) A visual, real-time hashtag tracker for Twitter, Instagram and Facebook.

Immediate Response Needed or You Lose

We have 36% less journalists than we had 10 years ago due to budget cuts and print media downsizing. Today's journalist (or blogger) is overworked, underpaid, and typically writing stories on borrowed time and tight deadlines. Over the past few years, I've jumped the fence from PR to journalism, and I can completely relate to being on a never-ending deadline. News moves fast, whether it's an evergreen story or breaking headlines. It seems like no matter what story I'm working on, I need immediate responses from sources, or I have no choice but to move on to the next source or idea.

Social PR Secret

Add live chat to your company newsroom or homepage so that a journalist/blogger—or anyone, for that matter—can get an immediate response while working on a story deadline.

Recently, I was writing a story and wanted to quote Krista Neher, CEO of Boot Camp Digital, and a leading authority on social media and digital marketing. I went to her website and saw her company offered a live chat on the website's media area and home page. Even though I know Krista, I needed to get some answers right away because I was on deadline. I typed my query into the live chat box and was able to get my answers with immediate response in a very social and visual way. Think about live chat as part of your website's PR strategy. With tools such as Facebook Messenger for Business and Twitter's customer service tools, it's becoming much easier to embed live chat onto our blogs, news sites, websites and more.

10 More Social PR Secrets For Media Relations

Journalists, bloggers, influencers and other spreaders of industry news are all on social media. So much so, in fact, that not including social media as a part of your Social PR strategy should be considered a drastic wasted opportunity.

To help you get your head in the social media PR game, here are top 10 quick and dirty social PR tips from social media marketing experts Ric Dragon and Lisa Buyer.

1. **Think like your audience.** Go sit on a mountaintop and meditate if needed; whatever it takes. But really get into your target audience's heads and endeavor to understand what content would mean something to them.

2. **Skip the self-promotion and find your common passion points.** The worst thing you can do is talk about yourself. Instead, consider what passion you share with your audience and talk about those. The people at Red Bull never talk about the fluid in the cans – instead, they talk about what their brand is *about* and the passion that connects the brand to the audience – people jumping out of helicopters; people living at the extreme.

3. **Build relationships.** In "old school" PR, we'd develop relationships with journalists; get to know them and what they were looking for. Today, it's no different. You don't need to go out there and connect with *every* journalist or blogger online – instead, just focus on building genuine relationships with the ones that are REALLY relevant to your endeavors.

4. **Create a scorecard.** Not all journalists or bloggers are going to have the same value for you, and neither are the things they might include you in. For instance, a mention in a blog post isn't going to have the same value as a feature article. So create a scoring system and target what you hope to achieve.

5. **Bring it offline.** Once you've developed a relationship with journalists online bring it offline. For instance, once upon a time a maker of luxury goods developed relationships with home and design journalists. After they hosted a meet-up of designers at the largest antiques show in the country, they ended up on a magazine cover.

6. **Your private messages aren't always private; If you can't tweet it, don't write it in an email or text it.** Your "private" messages can be forwarded, captured in screenshots and published in blogs, putting you and/or your brand at risk for public relations issues than can go viral in social media and cause irreversible damage in search results.

7. **Think like a reporter, write like a journalist and optimizes like a white hat SEO pro.** We are no longer speaking "spam-ish" or brochureware language. Get fluent in writing in a journalistic and topical style.

8. **Proactive policies now, mean less Social PR headaches later.** Be sure to have a social media policy in place for your brand, even if it is quick and simple like this one you can generate using Policy Tool (socialmedia.policytool.net).

9. **Be selfless to your community and brand advocates will follow.** You are not looking for a one night stand (*right?*), you are looking to build lasting and rewarding relationships. Play your part and the community will play theirs.

10. **Stay fresh, find inspiration.** If you run out of good ideas to write about, walk out of the office, jump on the treadmill for an hour (*like I did to write these tips when I was brain dead,*) meditate, or walk to Starbucks and read the WSJ. Do something other than stare at the computer and possibly publish something half-heated or self-serving. Remember, if you are

useless, your content will be useless. Make yourself productive and your content will be productive.[1]

Social PR Secret
"PSA for the world's PR people: Please stop calling me. Email pitches instead. If you don't hear back from me, I'm probably not interested." — Tweeted by The Washington Post opinion columnist Catherine Rampell (@crampell (twitter.com/crampell))

Public Relations Authority Rules, Tools, and Tips to Getting Quoted by the Media

Social PR Secret
The more often you are quoted by the media, the more likely you will be quoted in the future.

Today's media relations and research are more than press releases and mass email pitches; it's about being first, ranking in Google searches, social media mentions, and stand-out news content. Ever wonder how a journalist or blogger decides who to interview for a story and how they pick who makes the published final cut?

Some brands might think that the hardest part is getting the interview, but actually, once you have the interview, it's important to keep in mind that you are most likely not the only source, and the journalist/blogger might not use every source. You need to stand out and finish the race by actually getting published as the expert source in the story!

You have the interview—now what? The answer

---

[1] This article by Chelsea Adams originally appeared in the Bruce Clay Blog and was written by Kristi Kellogg http://bit.ly/1nLH5Ti

could be as easy as:

- Dare to be different. Thirty-five percent of experts interviewed are not quoted in the final story because the source says the same thing as everyone else.

- Say something out of the box.

- Don't play it safe by giving the same opinion as your peers.

- Share some incredible stats, blurbs, or predictions that will make your interview stand out from the rest.

- Provide third-party data paired with why you agree or disagree.

- Get visual. Having a curated library of images increases your chances of getting published and makes the media's job easier!

Watch for industry breaking news and provide a comment immediately to the reporters who typically cover that subject.

I want to be on the Today Show. *This is a perfect story for* The Wall Street Journal. *Why is my competitor always being quoted in* The New York Times *and I'm not?*

Getting quoted in top-tier media is no easy task, but the results create a credibility and authority factor that advertising can't match and can also result in natural links, the kind money can't buy and that Google considers a best practice.

History of the Media Choosing Experts

Up until the 1960s, a source's standing with journalists was determined by their political weight, which was a very reactive way to approach reporting. Politicians set the agenda, and that's what journalists would report. This eliminated the need for an

external opinion, so the only experts interviewed were "hard scientists" like biologists, doctors, and physicists.

Fast forward to the digital age; the Internet has made it necessary for journalists to adopt a new role. Now, they're interpreters
and analysts because merely presenting the facts to readers is not
enough. Journalists must explain *why* something happened and
what it means. It's no wonder the scientists that are most quoted
in articles today are social scientists who can explain the world
to readers.

In-depth reporting became the norm, and this required a more
critical approach to journalism. In came the experts. Erik Albaek
reports in his journal article "Experts in the Mass Media:
Researchers as Sources in Danish Daily Newspapers, 1961–
2001" that, between that time, the number of experts quoted in
print journalism increased sevenfold. A typical news story these
days also mentions more experts than it used to.

Say Hello to Natural Links

In addition to being considered an expert in your field, being
quoted in the media builds natural links to your website (the
ones Google likes!). Natural link building can amplify your
exposure, which in turn brings your audience to you and builds
your brand. It improves your search engine rankings and gives
potential customers a direct link to you. People prefer working
with someone who is well-known, and your quote has earned
you authoritative status—at least for your industry.

Search marketing experts Alan K'necht and Adam Proehl
declared that natural links are the best kind because your site
is getting talked about by real people. It's not the be-all, end-all
because you need more to get a targeted page to the top of Google search results for a desired keyword, but it should definitely
be a goal to acquire organic links.

How Journalists Choose Experts

Albaek's studies show that in more than 90% of cases, the journalist independently initiates contact with an expert source, and only a small amount of that is done based on a press release by the expert. That's not to say that press releases have lost their value; we just need to make sure they continue to be newsworthy and promote them in new and inventive ways.

Social PR Secret
Studies show that when journalists contact story sources,
those who have been used extensively in the past are used even more.
The more often you are quoted, the more likely that
will continue in the future.

The Rewards of Interview Originality

If you have a unique, original insight, then share it instead of saying whatever is expected. One may think that journalists call sources to confirm their own opinion but, in reality, they try to remove their opinion and only decide on the article's perspective after they have called one or more experts.

How to Increase the Odds of Being Quoted by the Media

One-hundred percent of journalists surveyed reported that they use Google as part of their story research. First and foremost, build your search and social presence! If you're already a renowned expert, then journalists will know to call on you, but if not, how do you suppose they'll:

a) find you and

b) consider you reliable enough to be worth getting in touch with?

If you want to be considered an expert, you need to start some type of authoritative content marketing. Write a blog, publish white papers, or, at the very least, create an industry-related account on Twitter and provide a running commentary on trends. Your best bet is a combination of these recommendations so that you can cross-promote and gain more ROI for the time spent working on them.

Tools to Track Media Mentions in Search and Social

- Google Alerts
- Mentions.net
- BrandMentions
- Topsy
- Crowdbooster

Remember, getting the interview is only part one of getting quoted by the media. Be sure not to miss an opportunity by being original in your interviews and the natural links will follow.

Chapter 3
The New Press Release

Today's press release is lighter, prettier, faster, and more than digital—it's electric news sparked by social media. It happens in real-time in 140 character snapshots or short-form videos from Vine, GIFs, and often bypasses traditional news outlets, originating instead from citizen journalists or inside brands.

Yesterday's static PR news was overweight—delivered in the form of a printed 400+ word press release or a bulky press kit filled with press clippings, photos, DVDs, and brochures—and written with the journalist in mind. Today's press release is the opposite of static. It's less, it's more, it's social, it's collaborative, it's fluid, and it's more visual and viral than ever.

Is the press release dead? I say it's evolving as part of this social PR revolution in which we find ourselves. Company news, brand experiences, and community engagement are morphing into storytelling. Journalists have an abundance of sources from which to gather information, but if you're on the frontline of social PR news content—whether a small business, large brand, or agency side—it's your job to influence the newsmakers and, as a brand, *be your own newsmaker* using today's evolution of a press release: visual story-telling content with your audience in mind.

In his keynote address at the Zenith Conference, Moz (formally known as SEOmoz) CEO Rand Fishkin stated, "The smartest brands will think and act like publishers."

With that in mind, the "monthly press release" has now morphed into many daily editorialized stories coming directly from the brand, curated by the brand and shared by brand ambassadors. Press releases can be counted in all shapes and sizes of newsworthy content published from a brand's:

- Website
- Website's company newsroom
- Corporate blog
- Live Streaming apps like Periscope, Facebook Live, Google+ Hangouts,
- Social media news channels (e.g., Facebook page, Twitter stream, YouTube channel, Snapchat Snaps, Instagram, etc.)
- Podcast
- Mobile apps
- Mobile news
  - 39 out of 50 news sites get more traffic from mobile devices than from desktop computers via Pew Research Center (www.journalism.org/2015/04/29/state-of-the-news-media-2015/pj_2015-04-29_sotnm_overview_01)
- Curated news publishing platforms (e.g., Paper.li, Scoop.it, etc.)
- Distributed Content Management Systems such as RebelMouse

Social PR Secret

Algorithms, trends and platforms change quickly, sometimes keeping you away from your primary focus: Great content. If you're looking for audience growth + engagement (who isn't?)- check out RebelMouse. They offer the first DCMS (distributed content management system) within an industry that orbits around social distribution.

In social PR, today's version of the press release is not always published by the brand. A brand's community can break news for the brand on behalf of the brand and faster than the brand. Companies like Whole Foods and AG Jeans let the brand's community announce news too, whether it's what beer is on tap today at the Whole Foods Beer & Wine Bar or what jeans just came in. By snapping visuals on Instagram or pinning ideas on Pinterest, the brand's community is reporting the news for us in many ways.

Influencer marketing can take the shape of sponsored blog posts; brand ambassadors; social influence programs such as Twitter, Instagram, or Snapchat; or branded entertainment on platforms such as Vine and YouTube. (from socialprchat.com/pr-under-the-influence-why-influencer-marketing-is-all-the-buzz)

A case in point example of influencer marketing in action is the company Lululemon, known for their athletic clothing and attire. The company often skims through their own online reviews to find customers who are enthusiastic and passionate about their products. If the consumer has a large social reach, such as owning a CrossFit studio, Lululemon may make an offer to them to become a brand ambassador. The CrossFit studio owner, for example, will share about his or her positive experiences with the brand while the studio gets exposure by Lululemon. Clearly, **it's a win-win relationship.**

But, there's still a place for the company press release—the process is shorter, there are more versions, and it's optimized for search and social.

Secrets to Writing Today's Press Releases

Today's successful social PR pros will find it is critical to not only be a good writer, but to also understand the basics of SEO and

SMO writing (source for more on SEM writing socialprchat.
com/seo-writing-secrets-for-social-media-the-bruce-clay-way).
Call it public relations optimization. I suggest stepping out of
the PR industry to find an educational source within the online
marketing industry. Some of my favorite educational search,
social and content marketing sources with quality resources,
instructors and platforms include:

- Boot Camp Digital (bootcampdigital.com)
- Bruce Clay, Inc (www.bruceclay.com)
- Cathy Hackl on Periscope (www.periscope.tv/cathyhackl)
- ClickZ Live (sesconference.com) (formerly SES Conference)
- Content Marketing Institute
- Copyblogger (www.copyblogger.com)
- Ekaterina Walter (www.ekaterinawalter.com)
- Peg Fitzpatrick (http://pegfitzpatrick.com/)
- Guy Kawasaki (guykawasaki.com)
- Heidi Cohen (heidicohen.com)
- How to Get PR for Your Start-Up by Murray Newlands (www.startupprbook.com)
- Joe Laratro's SEO Diet (seodiet.com)
- Moz
- PubCon (www.pubcon.com)
- Public Relations Student Society of America (PRSSA) (prssa.prsa.org)
- Razor Social (www.razorsocial.com)
- Search Engine Land
- Search Engine Marketing Professional Organization (SEMPO) (www.sempo.org)
- Search Engine Watch
- Social Fresh

- Search Marketing Expo (SMX) (searchmarketingexpo.com)
- University of San Francisco Online (www.usfca.edu/online)

4 Factors To Make or Break a Press Release

When a press release gets picked up, it's not by chance; press releases that get turned into stories are written with the editor and the journalist in mind. They're relevant, concise, engaging and error-free. Whenever you write a press release, cater to the sensibilities of journalists and editors—they're the ones, after all, with the power to turn your press release into an article. Use these factors to best leverage press releases within your digital marketing campaign.

1. Only Publish Truly Newsworthy Press Releases

Any time you issue a press release, consider whether the material is worthy of a news article. Is the information you're providing in the press release going to be relevant to readers? Is your press release the starting point of a high-quality article? If you can't answer yes to both of those questions, you shouldn't be writing a press release.

Social PR Secret
It's better to send out one press release a month that is substantial than four that are all fluff

Don't waste your time and the media's time with press releases that aren't newsworthy. Moreover, a brand that issues irrelevant press releases will lose clout among the editors and journalists who read it—and they'll run the risk of being ignored when they issue a press release that is truly relevant. Think the boy who cried wolf.

A newsworthy press release cover items such as:

- A grand opening
- A new product, service, book or program
- An upcoming event
- An award or recognition
- A donation or volunteer effort
- An acquisition
- Showcase an organization or company's employee as a go-to expert
- VIP hires or departures

2. Get to the Point and Be Concise

A press release should be between 400 to 600 words and the first line should get to the point straight away. Keep the following tips in mind, otherwise the journalist is *not* going to finish reading, let alone turn it into a story.

- Don't bury the lead
- Dispose of any fluff
- Resist the temptation to engage in hyperbole

A strong press release should open with facts and get right to the point. Here are two examples of the same press release. The scenario is the CEO of an investment company just published a new book and the company is issuing a press release.

Are you ready for the book that is going to change your life and revolutionize the way you invest? It's finally here! Throw every other investment book away and get ready to make money hand over fist.

Lame! Put yourself in the journalist's shoes. You have deadlines, time constraints, a desire to report real news, fast. If the introduction doesn't catch your attention, you're going to trash it.

Let's try this again… strip the jargon and focus on the facts.

Kinsey Group CEO Grace Kinsey shares her top investment tips and insights—based on more than two decades of experience; her latest book 'Financial Freedom 101' will be released by McRiley House next week.

In this second version of the press release, needless hype is disposed of and, in the first sentence, the reader understands exactly why this press release is coming across their desk. With a lead like this, you'll grab an editor's attention and possibly get your press release turned into a story.

3. Leverage Statistics, Quotes, Photos, and Videos

When journalists write a news story, it's laden with statistics, quotes and includes an image to engage their readers; in the same way, press releases that include statistics, quotes, and photos will engage the journalist.

Mickie Kennedy, the founder and president of eReleases agrees—in the "Beginner's Guide to Writing Powerful Press Releases (www.ereleases.com/offer/beginnersguide.html)," he advises brands to use statistics, noting that "statistics are an easy way to show the consequence or weight off something, and journalists often cite them to convey the importance of information."

Quotes from VIPs are also a strong addition to a press release, and often get pulled straight from the release and into the journalist's article. Whenever possible, include a quote from the C-suite.

Press releases should *always* include a graphic or video element. The demand for visual content hasn't just become huge for your fans on social media. It's also become essential for getting the attention of media outlets. Visuals can be the differentiating factor between a press release being used or not, especially if you organize it well for the media. In fact, 86% of all media is using outside-produced visuals and videos, so the better yours are, the more likely they'll pick them up! (source: socialprchat.com/new/2015/06/10/why-public-relations-and-seo-go-together-tips-truths-tools-and-faves)

4. Take the Format, Spelling, and Grammar as Seriously as an Editor Will

Believe it or not, some press releases are sent out with spelling and grammatical errors. Say goodbye to credibility! No journalists will take an error-laden press release seriously and, let's be real, if you didn't take the time to proof it, you're sending a message that they shouldn't take the time to read it.

Triple check your press release for spelling, grammar and formatting. Furthermore, make sure the press release is written in third-person and adheres to proper press release structure, including a headline, dateline, media contact and boilerplate—and bonus points for anyone who writes the press release in Associated Press (AP) style.

Social PR Secret
Grammarly is an online grammar checker that eliminates grammar errors, detects plagiarism and there's a Chrome extension for it. (www.grammarly.com)

When you write a press release, keep your audience's concerns at the forefront of your mind. Give your press releases a fighting chance to get turned into a story by keeping them relevant, concise, engaging, and error-free. These are the kinds of press releases that will grab the attention (and earn the respect) of the media.[2]

Social PR Secret

Go beyond reading an article on SMO and SEO writing. Get certified, and add some credentials to your social PR life.

It's called Public Relations Optimization. Take your social PR results to the next level and become proficient in writing quality titles, meta descriptions, and using natural links and keywords for all of your PR content. Your frequency of social PR content is paramount, just like frequency and timing of a magazine or newspaper. Wouldn't it be odd if *The Wall Street Journal* decided to skip a day? Plan for a news release or news content frequency of at least once a month and ideally two times a month or even weekly. It is getting to the point where brands will publish news content daily.

Social PR Secret

Write four or more versions of a company press release: one for paid distribution, such as PRNewswire that includes a photo, logo, and video; another version for the company blog which might be shorter, a little more casual and have a different visual; a website version for your online newsroom that varies slightly from the paid and blog version (add a 360 degree image or GIF!); and finally, social versions crafted with your brand's social network channels. This will help index more content with search and avoid possible duplicate content issues.

Visuals can make or break a story from getting shared or republished by top-tier media. Match an image—and if possible a video—with each press release, news release, article, or blog post. Studies show that including images and videos with a

---

[2]   Article Credit: This article originally appeared on the Bruce Clay Blog and was written by Kristi Kellogg bit.ly/1nLH5Ti

press release increases page views and search visibility, as well as increase your chances of getting picked up by a journalist. In a recent survey of 300 media professionals, 54 percent of journalists responded that they were more likely to review a multimedia press release than one that was entirely text. (source news.isebox. net/press-releases/2015-journalist-survey)

Social PR Secret
Break the press release up into 5 to 10 newsworthy Tweets with a link to the story on the corporate blog or company newsroom. This will send quality referring traffic to the full story.

Social PR Inspiration

In social PR, less is more, and visual is best.

Create a Facebook version of your news that is 50–100 characters (with keywords) or less with a strong image and a link back to the full story on your blog or website's newsroom or media coverage.

Make it pin-worthy! Even if you are not on Pinterest or Instagram, there is a good chance many of your customers are. Let them do the pinning or liking and sharing your news for you. Without a strong, inspiring visual to represent your story, the chances of your story or news getting pinned on Pinterest or noticed on Instagram become slim to none.

Snapchat Takeovers: For brands just starting out and trying to gain reach quickly, a smart Snapchat strategy is tapping into a Snapchat celebrity to do a "takeover". Cicero explains the steps on how to use Snapchat to grow your audience on the Delmondo blog. Add +NickCicero on Snapchat and subscribe to his newsletter for weekly updates on the latest and greatest Snapchat has to offer. (source socialprchat.com/5-snapchat-pr-secrets-digital-marketers-are-flocking-to-snapchat-are-you)

PDFs are great for many things, but not for press releases on your website. Don't post press releases or articles on your website in PDF format, as this does very little to help you get found by search engines like Google, which in turn reduces your chances of the media or your future customers finding you. All news and articles should be in HTML text format and optimized.

Check out press release publishing alternatives to share your news. Publish brand-centric or industry news, promotions, and more to new distribution platforms such as eReleases, Haiku Deck, or RebelMouse and bring your news content alive in the hands of your moving mobile market or fast-paced newsfeeds.

Social PR Secret
Pay attention to the types of links in a press release and make sure they follow Google's best practices and recent changes.

In today's content-fueled world, brands are moving far beyond hiring agencies to create ads and launch PR campaigns. Instead, we must venture to create newsworthy and authentic content—videos, blog posts, GIFs, Memes, Interactive Infographics, articles, apps, quizzes, games, comics, and other compelling digital content—built for news discovery and sharing. PR with compelling content is the future and it means the job as a publicist will become a lot more like that of a graphic designer, reporter, editor, or publisher and less like a "flacker." Today's social PR professional must create newsworthy and brand-centric content beyond the press that gets discovered by the right audience, captures attention, and compels people to share it.

Chapter 4
Content Strategy

First let's get one thing straight in regards to content: It's about *them*, not you. Once you understand that, you can read on.

What makes public relations such a power boost for social media and online marketing? PR secretly spells C-O-N-T-E-N-T, the kind of newsworthy content that Google loves and social media network users will share, like,♥, snap, pin, and follow.

Having a Journalistic Content Strategy

Early in my career, I was the first employee hired in the PR firm Boardroom Communications, which is now one of the leading PR firms in Florida. Julie Talenfeld, prior to launching into Boardroom Communications, was a TV reporter. I learned many things from Julie, but one of the most valuable things I learned was to write more like a reporter and less like a marketer.

Julie was—and still is—always looking for the newsworthy angle for her clients, the story that the audience will gravitate to instead of build the client's ego. Today's smart brands are taking a closer look at the quality, delivery, and channels of content and mirroring many of the traditional publishers' best practices: setting themes for days, creating special sections, stepping outside the brand's box, and including non-branded but relative content.

It's Not Me, Me, Me Anymore

PR used to be all about the "me, me, me" of a brand.

"Look at what we are doing and why it's so great. See who we just hired and why they're fantastic. We just announced a new product. We have a new partner who we think is important."

What is every headline in *The Wall Street Journal* started like this:

The Wall Street Journal announces…

That would get kind of boring and redundant. Eventually nobody would bother even reading any of the headlines.

Is that what your brand's online newsroom looks like? Do all the press release headlines start with your brand's name? That's boring, that's old-school, and that doesn't work anymore.

Who cares besides the brand? Really? Social media and self-published company news blogs allow the brand to take a positive editorial step outside the content box and offer up relative newsworthy content that supports the brand, but isn't always talking about the brand.

"Humans are seeking solutions to a problem," explains one of my friends and *Million Dollar Websites* author, e-business, social media, search and marketing expert, Rebecca Murtagh." Relevance is key. Framing communications in the context of how the new solution solves a specific problem can greatly enhance the value of the story. Proactively addressing key topics for target audiences (media, customers, investors, etc.) goes a long way in cultivating interest whether you write one general or three separate press releases.

Beyond the Press Release

Examples of Social PR-Friendly Content

- *Well-Written Blog Posts (with an author)*: Often, blogs are considered the nucleus of a social PR content strategy and can be a vital resource for customers, prospects, the media, and search engines.

- *Expert Guest Blog Posts*: They are a way of getting publicity in another publication. By writing a guest blog post, you position your brand as an expert source on another domain. Looking for guest bloggers or a guest post? Check out MyBlogGuest.com, a community by famed blogger, Ann Smarty, and keep in mind that guest blogging is an excellent way to reach new audiences, position yourself as an expert source, and build your brand.

  But be aware that guest blogging is no longer an acceptable SEO strategy and Google might penalize your domain. Read this article by Google's Matt Cutts, who was the head of Google's Webspam team, www.mattcutts.com/blog/guest-blogging/

  But here is an excerpt that underlines why guest blogging is still an effective branding and Social PR strategy:

  "There are still many good reasons to do some guest blogging (exposure, branding, increased reach, community, etc.). Those reasons existed way before Google, and they'll continue into the future. And there are absolutely some fantastic, high-

quality guest bloggers out there. I changed the title of this post to make it more clear that I'm talking about guest blogging for search engine optimization (SEO) purposes.

I'm also not talking about multi-author blogs. High-quality multi-author blogs like Boing Boing have been around since the beginning of the web, and they can be compelling, wonderful, and useful."

Matt Cutts on January 20, 2014 article on mattcutts.com

- *How-To Guides*: Use how-to guides as a social PR content strategy to show your audience how to learn something new, offering step-by-step tips.

- *Visuals*: With strong and powerful pictures, illustrations, graphics and interactive images, you better amplify your message, explain an idea, and gain user attention.

- *Infographics*: The infographic is one of the most popular forms of content marketing, and is an excellent alternative to explaining a complicated subject. However, avoid using them if most of your site visits are from mobile users.

- *Video*: Adding video to a press release, blog post, Facebook, Twitter, Instagram or other social media network posts increases the chance of engagements, interactions, a story getting picked up, website/blog visits, and more page views.

- *Illustrations*: Deliver news with a visual punch. Spending some time or money on illustrations to help report your news is a worthy investment. A humorous cartoon or a colorful abstract can go a long way.

- *Testimonials*: Let your happy customers share their stories. They serve as excellent social proof, third party credibility, and a boost to your social search results.

- *Case Studies*: This doesn't have to be an elaborate process; it can be a simple one-pager based on a template of information, or it can be customized and include a mix of multi-media and research.

- *Memes*: Pronounced "meem," it means something embraced, imitated, and shared by the online community as a whole. Memes are typically intended to make people laugh.

- *GIFs: Pronounced "JIF, like the peanut butter"* image files that supports both animated and static images

- *Email Newsletters*: This is old school meets new school. Email is still a leader in digital communications and journalists still favor email for pitches. Use email newsletters to round up news stories from your own blog, newsroom, and other third party sources.

- *eBooks*: If you've been writing a blog for a few years and have a pile of archives with relevant content, consider repurposing them into an eBook, and use it as a point of conversion.

- *Studies:* The published results of a detailed investigation and analysis of a subject or situation.

- *Cheat Sheets:* A reference tool that provide simple, brief instructions for making a decision or calculation, forming an opinion. This is like a mini-version of a guide, and in many cases is mixed with visual data.

- *Mixed Media Posts:* Mixing media such as images with audio, video, or animation that solve problems or answer a question can be effective, engaging, and highly promotable.

- *Social Promotions*: Sweepstakes, photo contests, surveys, and giveaways are paths to engagement and publicity generators. Check out platforms such as WooBox (woobox.com), Heyo (www.heyo.com), and Rafflecopter (rafflecopter.com), just to name a few.

Four steps to an effective social PR content strategy include:

1. Pick newsworthy topics and themes.

2. Write, create, and optimize, being sure to use keywords, hashtags, and Google's best practices in linking strategies. Check out ScribeContent.com, a content optimization platform for smarter content creation, social sharing, and search engine visibility.

3. Publicize and share.

4. Follow KPIs.

Social PR Secret

The key to magnetizing your Social PR content is effectively incorporating ALL three angles of relevance: Business Interest, User Interest and Time Significance as outlined below.

Angie Schottmuller, growth marketing and multi-channel strategist, came up with the triangle of relevance content strategy that matches perfectly with social PR.

Here is a graphic of it:

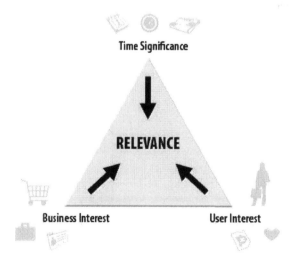

- *Business Interest*: The products, services, company mission, goals, or people relevant to the business or organization.

- *User Interest*: The goals, aspirations, pet peeves, turn-ons, values, hobbies, favorites, values, etc. of your target audience.

- *Time Significance*: Seasons, weather, holidays, life events (birthdays, anniversaries, etc.), major sporting events, current events, trending news and more. Present urgency, popularity, or seasonality. Why is this content relevant now?

Social PR Secrets Bonus Download

Download the Content Calendar—Triangle of Relevance (Excel Template) (www.convinceandconvert.com/wp-content/uploads/2011/03/Content-Calendar-Triangle-of-Relevance-Template.xltx) to get started.

"You can create the very best content in the world, but if no one can find it, then you've simply not succeeded. Digital PR is a heady mix between creating content and then optimizing it so that your audience can find it quickly and easily."
— *@DannyWhatmough, Chair of the PRCA Digital Group*

Once the type of content, timing, social media outlets, and PR media outlets are figured out, the next step is the social PR editorial calendar.

Chapter 5
Editorial Calendar

For centuries, traditional print publishers have used trusted editorial calendars—a schedule of what topics to cover and when—in some form to manage the publication of books, magazines, and newspapers. PR pros have also been using editorial calendars as a source when trying to pitch client stories to journalists and get stories placed. That was then, but this is now. Social media has dramatically increased a brand's number of owned media outlets, so smart businesses need to make the mental shift to think more like publishers. Managing content with an editorial calendar is a necessity.

While January might be the freshest time to fine-tune social PR planning habits, there's no time like now—as in today. One good place to start mapping out a schedule is the social PR editorial calendar.

For anyone who hasn't incorporated an editorial calendar into their social PR game plan, the primary purpose is to plan the publication or publishing of content across different media channels.

Remember that file you started last year and haven't opened since? It's been on your to-do list to share it and collaborate with your PR team. On the flipside, it could be a daily editorial master plan that you *did* follow that made your analytics go through the success roof. In the latter case, maybe it's a do-over or just a yearly update but without some sort of an evolving master calendar to serve as a guide.

Social PR Secret

Share your editorial calendar via Google Docs or Slack. Don't let it sit on your desktop. Editorial calendars are not an exercise, they are an action.

The Power of the Written Word

How can the power of the written word impact your social media and PR editorial calendar? Research (www.dominican. edu/dominicannews/study-highlights-strategies-for-achieving-goals) shows that people who write down goals, share that information with a friend, and send weekly updates to that friend are 33% more successful in accomplishing goals than those who merely formulate them.

If you consider your colleagues, subscribers, prospects, clients, and the media as "friends," think about the power of a written and organized social PR editorial calendar. Once you commit to a schedule and start publishing topical content on a consistent basis, your content will be fueled by the distribution and shares of your network.

Today's social PR editorial calendar takes into account web content, company press releases, blogs, and social media news network postings such as Facebook, Twitter, LinkedIn, Google+, Pinterest, Instagram, Snapchat, Live Streaming Apps such as Periscope and Tumblr, and YouTube, as well as email marketing plans and PPC (searchenginewatch.com/ppc) advertising should also wrap into traditional marketing campaigns.

Editorial calendars bridge together content and themes for social media, public relations, and beyond:

- Blogs
- Online newsrooms (bit.ly/1q8OVqb)
- Social media network messaging
- Events
- Email campaigns
- Video
- Offers
- Live conferencing
- Live hangouts
- Promotions and sweepstakes
- Web pages
- Seasons and Holidays
- PPC

Editorial Calendar Benefits

Social PR editorial calendars create a cohesive layer to a social PR content strategy that bridges the benefits of:

Accountability: Put it in writing. Cloud applications such as Asana (www.asana.com), Google Docs (drive.google.com), Slack (slack.com), or Dropbox (www.dropbox.com) allow collaboration where everyone can see it, touch it, and live it.

- *Commitment*: If you put a date on it, chances are you'll get it done.
- *Accomplishment*: Checking it off the list feels great and also ties back to accountability.

- *Planning*: Begin with big picture first, starting at the year, then month, then week, and then day. Knowing what will need to be done will save time.

- *Creativity*: Mapping out the topics first will help free space for creativity and inspiration.

- *Trends*: Tie in the topics with keyword research and boost the SEO (searchenginewatch.com/seo) strategy.

- *Measurement*: Watching the results in growth and also what is popular in content via tools such as Google Analytics will give you valuable information for future editorial ideas.

While an editorial calendar is a social PR must, remember to leave room for spontaneous opportunities. Navah Berg, a social PR marketing junkie, poetically says this on the topic:

"I find a lot of PR professionals set a schedule and follow it, sort of like a template; however, they fail to seize unforeseen opportunities like Oreo's newsjacking during the blackout at the 2013 Super Bowl that positioned the brand creatively in the forefront of news."

Social PR Secret
In the Social PR world, there is no such thing as a template. News can trend in a social media second, and we, as social PR pros, must always have our social PR game face on and be ready to play 24/7.

Tips for Creating an Editorial Calendar

Whether you're starting a fresh calendar or conducting a social PR makeover for your brand, the editorial calendar is mission critical for success. These tips are designed to inspire and motivate:

- *Set Goals*: Start with baby steps and grow in phases each quarter. For example, in the first three months, consider aiming to produce 40 pieces of social PR content total divided into blog posts and social media messages, and then set a goal for the second quarter to increase by 25%. Watch the analytics grow!

- *Frequency and Timing*: Break it down month-by-month, then week-by-week, and then day-by-day, even hour-by-hour depending on your resources and news cycle opportunity.

- *Themes*: Start with the overall brand strategy and choose topics or themes for each month into broad categories that can be broken down into sub-categories. One place to start is holidays, trade shows, seasons, fashion, sports, industry updates, etc. Another option is to dedicate each month to a different product focus or service of your company and design a collage of content ideas centered around that product or service in the form of videos, GIFs, social media posts, and blog posts.

- *Share, Play Nice, and Collaborate*: The social PR editorial calendar isn't designed to be a top-secret document. The idea is to share and collaborate across the team of writers, editors, researchers, and also the other departments such as SEO, advertising, public relations, product teams, and the sales team or even outside contractors.

- *Take Inventory*: Social media networks continue to evolve—many changes have occurred even in the past 6 to 12 months. As new social media networks and applications come into play, adjustments need to be made to accommodate these new messaging strategies. This is not an era to set it and forget it.

- *Social Mobile Messaging*: The explosion of smartphones, wearables and tablets brings new items to the social media editorial calendar for mobile users. Think about bringing in creative mobile messaging strategies such as location-based specials, beacons, QR codes, social offers, etc.

- *Voice Search*: The explosion of voice search makes podcasts and embedding the audio of your news into blog posts for more SEO juice easier.

- *Connect with Print Campaign*: Connect the dots between print and online and carry over print advertising themes and campaigns into the social PR calendar and vice versa.

Tools for Editorial Calendars

Organizing your editorial calendar is a matter of preference when it comes to format and what works best for your team. While I'm a very visual person, some love to use Excel and others prefer a collaborative platform. Figure out what works best across your team and go from there, fully expecting trial and error before finding the right solution. Consider some of these tools and platforms as a starting point:

- *Microsoft Excel* (office.microsoft.com/en-us/excel): This is the trusted standby and go-to solution that can be at least used as a first step in mapping out a strategy. I personally dislike Excel, but so many people live and breathe it that it is many times the first step in editorial calendar planning.

- *Google* (drive.google.com): Google makes it easy to set up editorial calendars using Google Calendar, Docs, Notes, etc., and it is easy to share.

- *WordPress Editorial Calendar Plugin* (stresslimitdesign. com/editorial-calendar-plugin): This gives the publisher a "bird's eye view" of your content, allowing you to control your long-term strategy. Celebrity copywriting stars such as Chris Brogan and Copyblogger give this plugin their recommendations.

- *HootSuite* (www.hootsuite.com): In essence, your social media editorial calendar is your dashboard of content broken down into timelines. HootSuite gives you that same dashboard feel when you break down the content into social networking messages.

- *21 Habit* (21habit.com): So you want to get your social media editorial calendar up and running in 21 days or less? Put yourself to the test with this app designed to help you make or break habits, whether they are marketing goals or other business and personal goals.

- *ContentDJ* (www.contentdj.com): Producing good content is just as important as curating good content. Check out the new kid on the block before your competition does.

- *Editorial Calendar Software by Marketing.ai* (www.marketing.ai/editorial-calendar-software.html): If you are an "in the cloud" type and like and online version with color coding that integrates with platforms such as HubSpot and Unbounce, this is for you.

- *Buffer* (bufferapp.com): This can help make your social PR content life easier by allowing you to schedule content, connect multiple accounts, post at the best times, and provide analytics to back it up. Buffer recently added new features such as feeds, analytics, and suggested content.

- *Edgar* (meetedgar.com): a social tool that allows you to build up a library of your content. You can put each piece of content into different categories within your library. Once you've built your content library, you can then create schedules across all your social media accounts and post out content to each one at specific times from specific categories. (Source: iag.me/socialmedia/reviews/how-to-become-a-content-marketing-jedi-with-edgar)

- *Slack* (www.slack.com): Collaborate with your team. This integrates well with Dropbox, Asana and countless other apps.

- *Asana* (www.asana.com): Also used a productivity tool, Asana enable teamwork without email and comes packed with a calendar feature that makes editorial calendar planning a breeze across multiple team members. It was founded by Facebook co-founder Dustin Moskovitz and ex-engineer Justin Rosenstein, who both worked on improving the productivity of employees at Facebook.

Social PR Secret
The simple application Buffer can be a secret weapon in bringing old blog content and news releases back to life and send new visits to otherwise dead pages. How? Once you get Buffer set up, go back to old evergreen blog posts and articles and share them (also called Buffering) for scheduled content after hours or on weekends.

Reporting on-the-spot news via social media is one way to get the word out. However, having an organized 12-month editorial calendar that divides the year into monthly, weekly, and daily snapshots can take your social PR content to new levels of success.

Social PR Secret
Working smarter in social media is a tough balance. Pplatforms such as ContentDJ or Buzzsumo help identify quality content and publish to social media sites and also come packed with social media editorial calendars to help with content publishing.

Chapter 6
Online Newsrooms

Legal blogger and attorney Roy Oppenheim is a partner of Florida-based Oppenheim Law. He uses an online newsroom as the hub for his firm's news, op-ed pieces, industry reports, blog posts, and social networks. But he also uses it as a way to communicate directly to the media and subscribers when news is posted. In turn, he reaches national and international media subscribers via email with his message and, as a result, gets media coverage in outlets such as *HuffPost Live*, *USA Today*, and *The Real Deal*.

What's trending? Online newsrooms. Call it the new "black," the must-have social PR communications tool that today's journalists expect, publicists-turned-content marketers need, and your organization's must-have website checklist.

Online newsrooms have been a staple of a corporate website's main navigation since the late 1990s—the static days of public relations and brochure-ware websites. However, today the online newsroom can be an organization's social PR secret weapon.

An online newsroom (also known as a pressroom, media room, press center, or media center) is the section within an organization's website domain that contains news related to the brand or its industry. Today's online newsroom is more than just a chronological list of press releases collecting digital dust—it's visited by not only journalists, but also customers and prospects. The online newsroom content is trolled by search engines and shared via social media. Online newsrooms are social, mobile, visual, and optimized as the news hub and one of the most-visited sections of a company's website.

Brands have never had more control and options to publish news and be the source of news, content, images, video, messaging, and it's a fact that the rapidly growing demand for online news continues to squeeze the traditional media. The public is demanding and expecting news faster, as it happens, with more visuals and easier-to-read stories.

Storytelling

Almost 100%[3] of journalists surveyed expect organizations small and large to:

- Have an online newsroom available to the media.
- Provide access to news releases within their online newsroom.
- Have PR or media contact information readily available within an online newsroom.
- Offer the ability to search news archives within an online newsroom.

Content and the Online Newsroom

Considering constant algorithm updates, online newsrooms updated frequently with quality news and content can only be a bonus for a company's branded online visibility.

---

[3]　　www.tekgroup.com

"The most critical element of any successful online newsroom is relevant and timely content." TEKGroup 2016 Online Newsroom Survey Report

More than 50% of journalists are visiting an online newsroom once a week and 64% visit one on a monthly basis.[4] Those numbers should motivate company newsmakers to deliver fresh content and package it in an organized and user-friendly way.

Size Does Not Matter

Expertise in a subject comes in all sizes, with 87% of journalists surveyed saying they visit both large and small-to-medium-sized organizations' online newsrooms.

Once known as the placeholder for archived press releases, today's online newsroom is command central for all company news activity and helps level the playing field for small companies to compete with Fortune 100 companies.

Make Your Newsroom Content Mobile-Friendly

Before you panic about your company's website not being mobile-friendly, check out this short checklist we put together to make sure your audience gets the most out of your company news on mobile:

Check your main newsroom's landing page and each press release page on a mobile device, so you can be aware of what your site looks like and what needs improvement.

This Google article will tell you all you need to know about optimizing for mobile! (www.google.com/webmasters/tools/mobile-friendly)

---

[4]   www.tekgroup.com

Make sure your press release pages are found by mobile users and that your audience knows you're accessible! You might even promote an update that your company's news can now be accessed through mobile, if it hadn't been before.

Online Newsroom Checklist

- *Social Media Networks*: Use social media to amplify your message. Make your organization's online newsroom your hub that lists all corporate social media networks. A social media landing page that contains access to all of your organization's social properties is also extremely important. 88% of journalists agree. (from TEKGroup 2016 Online Newsroom Survey)

- *Mobile Matters*: Ensure that your online newsroom is available in a mobile format to maximize your reach. Add responsive design to your list or look at a third-party platform!

- *Get Visual!* Let the statistics speak for themselves. Journalists prefer images and multimedia (so do people and search engines). Search results combined with an image have an increased performance and images or video are the most shared type of messaging on social media. 94% of journalists surveyed said that having photos in an online newsroom is important.

- *Vital Statistics*: It's really surprising how many organizations fail at incorporating the basic facts, background information, history, and milestones into the press center. More advanced content could include industry hot buttons such as trending issues and news, facts, and figures.

- *Multimedia Image Library*: Include logos, photos, images, videos (downloadable and embed codes), presentations, charts, and graphs. Editors, searchers, and search engines love this stuff, especially when optimized with image file names that make sense and using keywords, alt tags (text alternatives to images), correct file format such as JPEG, and offer a variety of image sizes!

- *Bios of Key Executives*: List names, titles, and photos of key management, with relative links to social media networks they belong to. Remember to save the file names of the key executive photos with the first and last name versus something generic.

- *RSS Feeds*: Today's searchers are savvy. Give them the opportunity to easily subscribe to your news and take it one step further by dividing news into categories.

- *Contact Information*: Although it sounds obvious, many times media contact information is missing or hard to find on press releases and online newsrooms. A 2013 online newsroom report by PressFeed (www.press-feed.com) states that just 10% of Inc. 500 companies have a contact name on the main page of their news content and an incredible 71% have no contact name on their press releases.

- *Featured News*: Make sure you have a section that lists most recent significant and relative media coverage, highlighting featured news at the top and using thumbnail visuals if possible. List it in reverse chronological order with a link to more detailed coverage.

- *Architecture*: Have the latest headlines showing on the newsroom home page and make sure the newsroom is easy to find on the home page.

- *Update Often*: The newsroom is an obvious place to add valuable, newsworthy, and relevant content to your website. This will yield fresh content for your visitors and increase your website's search authority.

Newsroom Sources

Online newsrooms are often on the wish lists of corporate communicators, but on the backburner for the development team. If this is the case, there are third-party online newsroom providers that can have your newsroom up and running in 24 hours or less, such as the following.

- TEKGROUP (www.tekgroup.com)
- PRESSfeed (www.press-feed.com)
- PitchEngine (www.pitchengine.com)
- Distribution services such as PRNewswire (www.prnewswire.com) also offer online newsrooms for companies looking to group news in one easy portal for journalists.

Social PR Secret

PDF press releases and all text press releases are OUT, so make sure your press releases are accompanied with a strong visual, such as an image, video, infographic, or chart. This goes for your press releases hosted on your own website's online newsroom.

Managing a brand's online newsroom opens up many search and social media doors for publicity.

The publisher, the editor, the producer, the research team, the photographer, and the fact finder—the social publicist wears many hats and must learn new talents in order to stay ahead. Read on to see what hat you will wear and when!

Chapter 7
The Art and Science of Social Publishing

Dan Zarrella will tell you there's a science to social publishing. After all, he's known as the award-winning scientist of social media and the author of four books on the subject. There are formulas, timing, and even linguistic analysis to social publishing. However, when it comes down to it, there is an art to it that sets your brand's content apart and makes you stand out in any newsfeed. It's the color, tone, shade, humor, sarcasm, timing, opinion, and commentary that spells success.

When you signed up for a Facebook Business Page, Snapchat or Twitter account, a new title came with it: *publisher*. Each social network you or your brand is connected to is like your own social publication. Think of your followers, fans, or friends as your subscribers and the quantity and reach as your circulation. Your most loyal brand advocates are most likely subscribing to all of your social channels.

What did your subscribers sign up for? Constant ads? No. Exclusive giveaways and promotions? Maybe. Quality content? Yes. They are looking for meaningful, newsworthy, inspiring, and remarkable news content tailored to them and you are their source for what matters in your overlapping world of likes and interests.

The Art and Science of Social PR

- *Keep social news messages short, sweet, and sticky*: For example, on Facebook, the first 90 characters are the most important.

- *Use strong visuals with your social news*: Photography, bright graphics, saturated colors, GIFS, infographics and memes that stand alone and work as a means to pull the reader in to view the message and ideally click through to a full story on your website or blog.

- *Write like a social news reporter and leave the selling out*: Avoid both extremes: on the one hand, gimmicky, sales-esque type of messages or, on the other, boring and plain messages that don't stand a chance in the highly competitive newsfeed of Instagram, Pinterest, LinkedIn, Facebook, Google+, or the fast moving stream of Twitter.

- *Write for the Retweet, +1, Share, Like (Reactions), Klout, Double Tap ♥, or Comment*: Facts, stats, tips, reports, studies, and breaking and trending news are good triggers for prompting a share. Ending or beginning a post with a question increases a post's impression and reach.

- *Avoid neutral messaging*: Studies show positive and inspiring messaging gets more engagement, shares, and interactions than negative messages. Meanwhile negative gets more engagement than neutral messages.

- *Video reporting*: Creating videos or live streaming on apps such as Facebook Live, Periscope, Google+ Hangouts, etc. and using them to report news is the pinnacle of storytelling. From a social PR angle, videos can be used for a quick report from the CEO, introducing a new product, or a how-to video that's easier to watch than read. A Vine, Twitter video, Facebook Live video, or Instagram video can be created for a second peek at a tradeshow or conference keynote, a behind-the-scenes tour of what happens at a law firm, a snippet of a yoga class, a happy scene at a Whole Foods event, a change in services, or a quick recap of a conference.

- *Sharing third-party content*: Reporting news with a share brings depth to your social PR reporting. Not every post can be about you, the brand, or a blog post by the brand. As part of the social PR content strategy, reporting news by sharing other like-minded content (and tagging them) brings goodwill and will position you as a news source.

- *Think SEO (search engine optimization)*: Optimizing content for search and social can increase visibility. Tastefully using branded keywords and phrases along with hashtags and tags can give your post a lift. Understand the basics of search and social optimization including keyword search, links, and meta descriptions.

- *Curating the daily news for your community*: Save your community time, and be a resourceful means of getting the news and information for your industry. Sarah Evans does a great job at this with her daily Faves + Co email (formally #Commentz) email that gets plugged into her social networks. One of her taglines is "I do the research, so you don't have to." Another example is Mashable; they swipe the news and package it back to you in one easy-to-read email of the top headlines.

- *Pull Social PR Rank*: Position yourself as an expert source, an authority on a topic and stand out as an author in search results. If you're writing for your company blog, guest blogging, or contributing to a publication, it's a social PR competitive advantage to establish a level of influence. Check out ClearVoice for some actionable authority steps.

- *Join a Google+ Community (or, even better–create one)*:
  Socialize, mix, and mingle with a like-minded community
  and share expertise, questions, answers, and even news!
  Hangout, Google style.

- *Every Story Becomes a Pin (and a Referring Link)*: Your
  news articles, media coverage, blog posts, and videos
  are all as Pin-worthy as they are newsworthy! Create
  "Pinterest"ing boards centered on different categories of
  your news and make sure to pin each story to its relative
  board. Note: Don't forget to optimize the pins and board
  descriptions with keyword-rich content along with
  hashtags.

- *Pin-Worthy Images*: The rise of visual social media
  marketing makes each image selection for a blog post
  critical and dictates that you must match each press
  release or media coverage recap in the company online
  newsroom with an outstanding visual. Your article,
  blog post, and news release must be accompanied by a
  pinnable image to get your social PR news shared in the
  visual network of Pinterest.

- *Keywords*: Did I mention optimization? If you want your
  content to be found in a search on Facebook, Twitter,
  LinkedIn, YouTube, Google+, Pinterest, Instagram, etc.,
  then you must include the relative and unique keywords
  in the news messaging.

  Here's an example:

  Wrong: "Our awesome pizza is half price for the next
  hour."

  Right: "La Gondola Chicago-style pizza is half
  price for the next hour at our Ashland location.
  #NationalPizzaDay"

- *Hashtags*: When reporting news within the social
  networks that support hashtags, make sure to include

the relative and trending hashtags to boost your potential visibility. For example, if you're at a conference, make sure to use that hashtag to report a trending topic or event such as the #grammys (twitter.com/search?q=%23grammys&src=typd).

Social PR Secret

For maximum clicks on Twitter, place your link about 25% of the way through the Tweet (versus at the end). Dan Zarrella found these Tweets had a higher CTR (Click Through Rate) as reported in The Science of Marketing (amzn.to/1p4ojHb).

Chapter 8
Managing a Community

I can promise you this: no two days will ever be the same for a social PR pro turned community manager, and time management will always be an issue.

Do yourself a favor and read Peter Bregman's book, *18 Minutes: Find Your Focus, Master Distraction, and Get the Right Things Done* (peterbregman.com/18minutes). I highly recommend it for anyone in the social media and public relations business. The book was a result of a blog post Bregman wrote for the Harvard Business Review that became one of the most popular and most commented posts on the site. That post, "An 18 Minute Plan for Managing Your Day (bit.ly/1vIIKBL)," began with Bregman's humble admission that we can all relate to. Here's my slightly modified version:

> *"Yesterday started with the best of intentions. I walked into my office with a keen sense of what I wanted to accomplish. I sat down with my laptop and a Starbuck's latte, checked my streams in Instagram, Facebook, Twitter, Google+, and email. Two hours later, after fighting several digital fires, solving other people's PR problems, and dealing with whatever happened to be thrown at me through my social PR world, I could hardly*

> *remember what I had set out to accomplish. I'd been ambushed*
> *at social media gunpoint. And I thought I knew better..."*

Below, I've taken Bregman's principles and applied them to a day in the life of a social PR professional.

The 18-Minute Social PR Day

Step 1 (5 Minutes): Your Social PR Morning Minutes: This is your opportunity to plan your social PR for the day. Before turning on your computer or picking up your smartphone, sit down with your to-do list and decide what needs to happen to make this a successful day. Determine what can you realistically accomplish, whether it's writing a blog post, researching a new Twitter tool, sitting in on a webinar, or getting ready for that next conference. If you have crossed the digital bridge and *must* turn on the screen versus using paper, then check social media calendars in your Google Docs, project management in Basecamp, Asana or get social and collaborate in Slack.

Step 2 (1 Minute Every Hour): Social Media Refresh and Refocus: Managing your social media time hour-by-hour is both a discipline and a science. Don't let the hours manage you. How many times do you suddenly realize you have spent the last 20 minutes reading Twitter updates, Snapping away on Snapchat, thumbing Facebook Pages, Regramming an Instagram image, or reading an article from an email subscription? Set your phone, laptop, or Apple watch to ring every hour and start the work listed on your calendar. When you hear the beep, do a social media checkup. Assess your progress, and recommit the next hour to getting back on track. Momentum inspires you to be more productive. Set a daily focus and eliminate distractions with this Google Chrome extension: chrome.google.com/webstore/detail/momentum/laookkfknpbbblfpciffpaejjkokdgca?hl=en

Step 3 (5 Minutes): Your Social Media After Dark: At the end of your day, shut your laptop and review your social PR day. Ask yourself some questions: "How did my social media day go?" "What did I learn today?" "With whom did I interact?" "Did I meet new followers on Twitter that I should send a quick @ reply?" "Was there a nice RT of me I should acknowledge?" "Are there any comments on my blog I should respond to?"

Building and maintaining relationships is critical in social PR, and it's easy to forget that it takes just a few minutes to share appreciation, congratulate someone, or offer thanks.

All that seems easy, but here are some tips to add to the 18-minute plan.

- *Social Media Delete*: It's very hard to say no. All of these unscheduled things can rob you from important and strategic social media time. To get the right things done, choosing what to ignore is as important as choosing what to focus on.

- *Schedule the Hardest First*: Bregman emphasizes (but it is really hard to always do) placing the hardest and most important items at the beginning of the day. He also notes the power of "when" and "where." Studies show that when you schedule an action item with a time and date, the chances of it getting done are far greater than letting it float. No meetings in the morning!

- *Balance Connectivity. Social PR Community Managers Connect with their Community*: Being on the frontlines of your social media news channels can be a cross between a reporter on a breaking news desk and a community hotline. A traditional newsdesk is constantly looking for tips on breaking news to cover and also juggling the daily programming. A community hotline is on the frontlines and never knows what type of question and comments might come up for moderation and advice.

PR professionals wear many hats, including event planner, crisis manager, spokesperson, newsmaker, graphic designer, search engine optimizer, videographer, and more. And, with the influx of social media, they have the right to claim authority and ownership as social media community manager, or at the very least, part-time manager or moderator. Part-time or full-time, there is no time like the right time to pull community management under the social PR umbrella in some way, shape, or form.

After all, when a community fight, blunder, or issue comes up, guess whose problem it becomes? *"Hello, this is the Community Manager calling for PR Manager, we have an issue on Facebook..."*

Salesmen to the Left

Malcolm Gladwell coined the term "connector" in his book *The Tipping Point: How Little Things Can Make a Big Difference.* Connectors are people who love networking and are all about making change happen through people. Gladwell describes connectors as those people who know many worlds and can link people to networks they did not know existed.

Social PR Secret
Connectors make savvy Social PR Managers. Salesmen do not.

What Does it Take to Be a Social PR Community Manager?

- Yearning to learn. In the digital world the only thing that is constant is change.

- The love of sharing and connecting resources.

- The art of listening. Listening is a natural skill. What is your community telling you?

- Empathy: be able to put yourself in the shoes of the person who is talking to you.

- Editorial skills and a reporter's mindset: sniffing out the story with a journalistic flair and voice.

- Customer service: superpowers to squash, handle, and acknowledge issues and concerns.

- The ability to be calm, cool, and collected.

- Fast, multitasking madness with organizational skills.

- A sense of humor.

- Judgment: on the frontlines of social PR community management, it's important to be able to call the shots in real time and make sure they're the right ones.

- Conversation: you need to know how to attract people to you and create actions within your community in an authentic way.

- In touch: being caring and responsive.

- Resourcefulness: thinking outside the box.

- Visual: you could call yourself a "creative director wannabe."

Social PR Secret

Read The Complete Social Media Community Manager's Guide (amzn. to/lov399k) by Marty Weintraub and Lauren Donovan. It's not a skinny book, but it'll be your go-to source for all the essential tools and tactics for social PR community management success—and beyond.

Chapter 9
Dialing Into Social PR Customer Service

Social Customer Service

Social media is the new 1-800 number. It is all about mindful listening, intentional personalization, speed, and connections. And not just personal connections, but also the conversations happening around your brand. How can public relations be a customer service win for your brand? First, we need to understand how social media, public relations, and customer service connect.

Is customer service important? Of course, ask any brand.

80% of companies say they deliver "superior" customer service but only 8% of people agree with them. Now this: 66% of consumers expect a response on social media within an hour and

56% of consumers want a response within 30 minutes. The reality: Social media does not have a hold button. Your customers want immediate gratification. They are no longer calling or emailing customer service, they are Tweeting, messaging, and sharing problems and opinions in their newsfeed and directly to your social media networks.

"It doesn't matter if your company is one person, or a million people. People want to know they matter. They want to know they are listened to. And the best (and only way) to do that is by actually doing it," Peter Shankman notes in the introduction of his book *Customer Service: New Rules for a Social Media World.*

Press 2 for customer service. *Now, wait on hold for 45 minutes.*

Go to our website and contact us right away. *First click through 5 pages to find the right email.*

Send an email for customer service inquiries. *We'll get back to you in 5–10 business days.*

Chat with us online. *We're sorry; nobody is available at this time.*

Follow us on Twitter. *Sorry, out to lunch, please Tweet again later.*

Like us on Facebook. *Our social media manager is out sick today, please leave a message.*

It's amazing to think of the hoops that some brands make their customers go through just to get a simple question answered or a problem solved. Isn't public relations all about dealing with the public? But what happens when we mix in today's social-savvy customers looking for instant gratification—or else?

Or else what? They move on to your competition, leave a scathing review on Yelp, turn to a complaint website such as Rip Off

Report, and then your online reputation is tarnished, which turns into a much larger public relations problem.

So why not avoid all this potential damage and be proactive by taking your customer service in your Social PR hands. When clients ask me how to best avoid getting negative search results or social media mentions, my first answer is to be proactive in getting positive search results and positive brand mentions or reviews. The same holds true for customer service. Make as many happy customer experiences as possible from the beginning, so when the bumps come in the customer service road, you already have a positive social media footprint.

The Social PR and Customer Service Connection

What's a Social PR pro to do? It's impossible to ignore the social customer when it comes to mapping out a social media and public relations strategy. The larger social platforms such as Facebook and Twitter continue to emphasize and support brands in the use of social media for customer service.

Listening

Studies show people feel better when they feel listened to and that listening can be applied to social media as well as in real life. Less talking and more listening. The bottom line is people want to feel heard. Once they feel heard and empathized with, they will often calm down and their huge problems often become smaller. We feel even better when we feel understood. To be understood, we must be listened to. Often, it is more important to us to feel heard than to actually get what we said we wanted.

Track Brand Mentions

The only way you can let people know that you are listening is to make sure you have all your tools in place to track when your audience is talking about you. Just like we monitor brand mentions using Google alerts, it is a best practice to monitor any brand mentions to know who is talking about you on social media. More than just monitoring when your brand is tagged, brand mentions include company names, product names, and even business owners, senior executives and founders.

Track @mentions, hashtags, and brand names with tools such as Sprout Social, Mentions, or even Tweet Deck to monitor who is talking about you

Be Real

Personalizing your messaging is key to social customer service. The last thing people want is to get the feeling they're receiving canned responses in a robotic manner. It's called *social* media for a reason, so be social and more relaxed than formal emails and conversations.

Is it okay to be prepared with guided answers to FAQs for customer service? Definitely. But make sure you give them flexibility to personalize with some examples of tone, voice, and brand personality. Emojis can be an effective way to offer some humanization and emotion behind customer service messaging, just be sure to keep the business side first and not get too over the top.

Set up an Infrastructure

One of the first steps in getting organized for social customer service is to have a solid infrastructure in place to monitor messaging, resolve issues, and provide a seamless customer experience, one that allows the best possible collaboration across different teams and two-way communication. This can be challenging, especially since many brands are challenged with "border patrol" between departments which happens when departments work in isolated teams and don't communicate and collaborate.

SparkCentral, Sprinkl, Hootsuite, and SproutSocial make it possible for companies of sizes to integrate some form of customer service dashboard with social listening and social customer service.

Deal with Negative Feedback ASAP

Complaints and problems that are ignored only turn into bigger complaints and problems. Negativity spreads like wildfire on social media and the problem is that the stickiness of most of the content tends to haunt a brand longer than anyone would like turning one overlooked conversation into a public relations nightmare. Complainers are complaining for a reason: They want to feel heard.

While we only wish the world were full of rainbows, lollipops, and unicorns, the reality is that it's the negative feedback that usually helps us grow, learn, and refine. The catch is to make sure that negative feedback is handled quickly. The faster the response time, the better the chances of earning back a customer's trust and business.

Stay in the Platform

The reason that customers turn to platforms such as Twitter and Facebook to file a complaint (or positive review) is out of pure convenience. It's quick, easy, and usually they can do it while in transit to the airport or waiting in line at the grocery store. As a brand, we need to keep it easy for them and try our best to take care of the issue within the platform they used. For example, on Twitter, you can easily go from a public Tweet to a direct message (DM), and on Facebook, you can easily go from public comments to Facebook Messenger.

Respect Customer Privacy

As social conversations happen across social media, it's a no-no to over-share your customer's private information, especially things like:

- Email address
- Home address
- Phone number
- Credit card
- Children's names
- Social Security number

Respond Quickly

A fast response. That's the number one thing your social customer wants (this includes the media). Period. End of story. It is more important for customers on social media to receive a fast response than an accurate response. Crazy, right? But true.

There is a definite need for speed when it comes to social customer service. Again, this all goes back to listening and monitoring. We can't be a first responder if we don't hear the calls for help on social and have a team (even if it is one person) dedicated to acknowledge and direct the message to a path to resolution. You don't have to be an airline to make customer support a priority; social brands like Buffer and Moz take social service very seriously.

"Customer support" is something of a magic phrase at Buffer, according to Content Crafter and Culture Creator Courtney Seiter. In this article, she wrote, "Simply put, it's one of our very favorite things to talk about and improve upon every day. Customer support is baked into everything we do—Buffer's vision is to build a super-useful social media management tool with amazing support for everyone we come into contact with."

Buffer's name for customer service reps is nothing traditional. They call themselves Happiness Heroes, and I can say firsthand that they make me smile every time I have a problem (which is not often).

Random Acts of Kindness #FTW

Taking customer support on social media one step beyond the ordinary is a smart strategy that many brands overlook. The art of the handwritten thank-you note is one simple and affordable way to go above and beyond and get personal with customers using random acts of kindness for the win. An attitude of gratitude often gets shut down and stomped out in this fast and furious digital business world. Brands worry more about putting out fires and less about nurturing and growing a relationship beyond the point of resolution.

Turn Complaints into Content

Listen to the conversation. Is your audience complaining or wishing for something in your industry? Address it with content. For example, maybe the consumer doesn't know how to clean their at-home Starbucks Coffee Maker, and it's been notated a few times on social. Create a "how to clean" video. Remember, social selling occurs when companies align customer service with marketing and sales.

Influential Brand Mentions

Influencers can make your brand or break your brand. Manage it with social listening tools and be sure to notice the attention when an influencer—journalist, blogger, celebrity, evangelist, investor—talks about your brand. Be proactive, and find your influencers. Reach out to them before they have to reach out to you or before your competition beats you to the punch.

Social Synergy

TEAM: Together Everyone Accomplishes More. PR and customer service are both problem solvers. Working together on messaging is important. PR's knack for content, and customer service's "No problem" attitude, can create a positive experience from an unhappy customer.

Customer service is good for PR.

Sometimes the Truth Hurts—Or Not

An eye-opening example of staying true to your brand is an example of when a Yelper posted a one-star review for a dive bar and how the owner shot back a brilliant and risky response that landed some positive media attention. Not every brand can get away with this, but the customer service team working closely with PR can turn a negative Yelp comment into a PR win. mashable.com/2016/01/19/dive-bar-yelp/#SZWYoWg1KOqw

Social PR Customer Service Tip
Make sure you hire highly skilled communicators to run your social media channels, ones that are empathetic and compassionate.

Mindful Measuring

Tracking the social customer service progress is a best practice to really monitor and report on success as well as learn from mistakes. Keep track of social inquiries and your responses. Do you use a customer service platform? What type of messaging are they using—live posts, tweets, hashtags, trends, or direct or private messages?

Are you able to easily track and escalate issues behind the scenes, yet still respond to the customer in the space where they have contacted you?

Social Media + Customer Service + Public Relations = Real-Time Drama

It can be exciting, scary and sometimes entertaining. We can take a negative experience from a consumer and turn them into a social media influencer with the right timely strategy. The bottom line? Don't just respond, have a strategy in place and communicate it with your social response team. Though speedy responses are needed, it's much more important to stay on brand and zero in on what is highest priority and what is lower priority.

As social media channels grow up and mature, the customer also becomes more sophisticated and their expectations increase. Facebook and Twitter have both made significant investments in making customer service tools available to brands.

Taking Social PR cues from social customer service.

Facebook

Facebook takes social customer service seriously and continues to invest in making the best experience possible for brands and users to communicate on the platform. The Facebook Pages along with Business on Messenger lets businesses integrate into the chat app and communicate directly with customers. Response times, customer badges and redesigned inbox's make it easier for businesses to manage customer service.

Twitter

- Businesses can now add a deep link to their Tweets that automatically displays a call-to-action button, which allows the customer to send the business a Direct Message, quickly and easily.

- Direct messages have been expanded to more than 140 characters making it easier for usrs to communicate privately with brands

- Twitter Polls are a great tool to get customer feedback on a new product development

- Twitter's latest customer service-specific tool is a feature called Customer Feedback. This lets people privately share their opinions with a business after a service interaction.

- **Stat:** According to Twitter, millions of customer service-related interactions happen on the platform every month and many advertisers report that over 80% of their inbound social customer service requests happen on Twitter. (Example. (https://g.twimg.com/blog/blog/image/NPSFeedbackhalf.gif)

Instagram

Use hashtags to create a community around your posts. Hashtags can help you reach the consumers who are most likely to be interested in what you have to say. But make sure to use them strategically and sparingly instead of just jumping on the latest trendy tag.

Snapchat

- Text message: allows users to have conversations, rather than just sending individual photos and video messages. Brands can have lengthy conversations with customers in a direct, private messaging style. One small business using Snapchat for customer service is Gainesville-based Scooters 4 Less. Owner Collin Austin reports using Snapchat's chat feature to communicate with its college student customers after hours and even conducts some initial interviews via the video chat feature.

- Live video chatting can only occur when both users have the Snapchat app open and are in the same conversation. This is an opportunity for brands to utilize the video chatting option to connect with users for a face-to-face exchange.

Customer Service Listening Tools

- **Paid:** Lithium, Radian6 from Salesforce, Brandwatch, Spredfast, Conversocial, FalconSocial, Freshdesk, www. icerocket.com

- **Free:** Mention in combination with Feedly, HootSuite in combination with TalkWalker app (popular and free), Nimble (ROI of social analytics), Google Alerts, HootSuite in combination with TalkWalker app. Twitter Notifications: twitter.com/settings/notifications

- **Influencers:** BuzzSumo to find out what's trending, who the influencers are in your industry, and which of your content gets the most engagement.

Tip:

Import Your Mention updates into Feedly, details here: blog. bufferapp.com/social-listening

To pull your Mention alerts into Feedly, click on the RSS icon in your Mention account (found in the "Settings" section under "Manage my alerts.") Copy the URL from the popup.

Chapter 10
Jump Into Any News Story

Some call it newsjacking—a term made famous by David Meerman Scott in his best selling book, *Newsjacking: How to Inject Your Ideas into a Breaking News Story and Generate Tons of Media Coverage* (amzn.to/1sTR6AW)—where he describes how the traditional PR model of sticking closely to a preset script and campaign timeline no longer works the way it used to. Say hello to social media and real-time news! The idea of newsjacking is to inject your news into what is breaking or trending, making yourself part of the story and generating media coverage for yourself or your organization.

The term newsjack sounds harsh—like hijack or carjack. A nicer way to say it might be "news lift," where news is used to lift a story on your behalf and hopefully add value to the audience.

There are a variety of situations in which a brand can break into a news story, such as:

- Sensational
- Tragic
- Disaster

- Commercial
- Breaking
- Seasonal
- Sports
- Celebrity
- Political
- Legal

Making sure that your trusted social PR editorial calendar has flexibility and agility is important to take advantage of or adjust your news stream to accommodate relative news.

Write Yourself Into Any Story!

This can be done strategically, swiftly, and easily using the publishing platform of your social media news networks. Here's some advice:

- Pay attention to breaking news.
- Understand the keywords being searched in a particular news cycle.
- Produce high-quality, well-researched content that serves a specific demand for information.
- Quickly syndicate your injected news over social networks to be found when other news organizations search for sources.
- Rewrite and edit the titles and descriptions.

More Secrets

- Comment on a news story in a top-tier publication or industry blog: reporters, editors, and bloggers pay attention to these comments and will look for expert opinions in future stories.

- Comment on Twitter news from the reporter with an authentic personal note. For example, "I agree," "Great story," or "Interesting and well-written."

- Retweet a story with an opinion or original twist.

- Facebook: you can share a story from *The Wall Street Journal* and customize the title and description to make yourself part of the story and inject your opinion.

- Write an opinion or editorial piece as a guest columnist or blogger commenting on a story.

- Do a Blab and invite others to talk about the topic. Download the video and upload bits of it to social and add the full video on YouTube, then embed it to your blog!

- What's the best tone? Positive works better than negative or controversial, but controversial or negative works better than neutral according to recent research by Dan Zarrella.

A Few Rules

- Recognize that unlike traditional PR, newsjacking is real-time and fleeting, so your timing is critical.

- Be sure the story is related to your target market or industry.

- Ask for links when working with a blogger, editor, or reporter as an expert source on an opinion of a trending or breaking story. Links from authority media outlets can drive quality traffic to your website our blog and also add value to the search engines.

- Share the story on social and tag the reporter, not just the brand.

- Acknowledge the reporters.

- Content comes first. PR comes second.

- Use social media for quick dissemination and viral spread.

Good Sources

- Google Alerts (www.google.com/alerts)
- Breaking News (www.breakingnews.com)
- Buzzsumo (buzzsumo.com)
- Talkwalker (www.talkwalker.com/alerts/login)
- Google Trends (www.google.com/trends/explore)
- If This Then That (ifttt.com)
- Twitter Text Alerts
- Newsle (www.newsle.com)
- CNN Reports (www.cnn.com)
- Mention.com (mention.com/en)

Trending but Predictable

Events, campaigns, holidays, or activities that are already planned are an easy option to consider when looking for news to make yourself part of a trending news story. Events such as The Academy Awards, VMAs, Breast Cancer Awareness Month, or your industry's annual surveys and reports work great. Even holidays such as Valentine's Day, Thanksgiving, and Independence Day can trigger bursts of news opportunities. Predictable events such as the Super Bowl can also be perfect for breaking news opportunities such as the infamous blackout and halftime "wardrobe malfunctions."

Breaking News

- Celebrity gossip such as Kim Kardashian's marriage, divorce, nude selfies, and pregnancy

- Social media brand blunders

- Verdicts, such as the Casey Anthony sentencing

- Tragedy, as in the Malaysian Airlines flight or Boston bombing

- Sports wins or losses, like in the Super Bowls

- Political faux pas when nude selfies or drunken banters make it to the mainstream media

Social PR Secret
Have your team ready and assigned to predictable large events as your social PR reporters waiting for that breaking story to newsjack and make your own.

For example, Oreo has a team of brand executives and social media staff including writers and designers ready to jump on an opportunity to pull social PR rank, and they did with a touch-down of a Tweet.

At around 9:00 p.m. on a Sunday night, Oreo tweeted, "Power out? No problem." Since then, it's been retweeted more than 15,000 times (and the same image on Facebook has received more than 21,000 likes and almost 7,000 shares), meaning that the most powerful bit of marketing during the advertising industry's most expensive day may have been free. That's smart social PR.

David Meerman Scott's Newsjacking Wisdom

In a recent interview for my class at the University of Florida, David Meerman Scott offered his top do's and don'ts when it comes to newsjacking. Stick to these tips to become a newsjacking pro, but proceed with caution so you don't end up being a cheesy news hijacker.

Do's of Newsjacking

Do Utilize Blogs because they will be indexed by the search engines.

The act of newsjacking can be accomplished with a simple tweet or post on another social media platform. But, if you're first on the scene and have a great angle to share or contribution to make, stop what you're doing and write a blog!

A blog allows more people to view your content if they are searching for a specific news story on a search engine. After a while your tweet will be bumped down by the constantly-moving newsfeed but someone doing a browser search will see your article as the odds are there are less people taking the time to do a writeup.

Do Be Quick

Scott says "you can't wait until tomorrow, you probably can't even wait a few hours."

When breaking news happens, it is crucial that you add in your own content as quickly as possible. The newer a story is, the more people will be searching for it. This means the sooner you post, the better chance you have of the most people viewing your content.

Don'ts of Newsjacking

Don't Newsjack Death and Destruction... *and be very careful with religion sex and politics.*

These are often very sensitive topics that can easily cause offense if taken out of context. It is best to avoid these altogether if possible. A newsjacking example would be the story during the 2014 World Cup of the player from Uruguay who would bite his competitors. Can you imagine how great would that have been for a company selling baby teething toys? I imagine the blog headline would read "Luis Suarez Bites Other Players But Your Child Won't: 3 Ways To Stop Children Biting" or something to that effect.

Keep in mind there is a fine line between newsjacking for a brand's commercial gain and a acknowledging news because it strikes a personal chord or has a legitimate news tie with your personal or business brand. For example, the crushing news of Robin Williams' untimely death swept across social media and traditional news like an avalanche with mostly very genuine and heartfelt tributes with legitimate connections, this is not newsjacking, this is being real, authentic and human.

Don't Spam Hashtags!

If you are going to newsjack a hashtag from Twitter, make sure that it is relevant to your business or your content. You have to be adding value to the hashtag or the conversation.

Scott, for example, says when someone else is talking about newsjacking at a conference he will wait until the session is half-way through and he will tweet about a blog post regarding newsjacking with the conference hashtag! The people at the conference can't believe that their session attracted the man who wrote the book and it's a win-win. Scott gets more exposure without taking over the conference hashtag by being genuine and news-jacking at a strategic time.

This version of newsjacking has also been referred to as "hashtag hijacking" and can work really well (referring to the conference example above) or more like a hijacking crash and burn. It is a dangerous tactic that has the ability to disrupt the harmony of Twitter when abused by brands sales messages. For example, when Kenneth Cole's Twitter account used the trending hashtag #Cairo completely out of context.

The brand posted this Tweet during the protests in Cairo in 2011, an extremely serious event. "Millions are in uproar in #Cairo. Rumor is they heard our new spring collection is now available online at bit.ly/KCairo -KC." I'm sure you can see why this form of "newsjacking" does not fall under Social PR best practices.

Chapter 11
Distribution, Amplification, and Promotion

Distributing your company's news has a whole new meaning since the days of messenger services, U.S. mail, fax machines, and old-fashioned wire services. The first press release dates back to 1906, and in 1954, PR Newswire was first to create a system for electronic distribution of news releases. Prior to its establishment, companies issuing press releases to the New York media had to messenger, dictate, or mail each copy of their news releases to the city's daily newspapers and news services.

With the advent of PR Newswire, companies were able to send a single copy of their news release to PR Newswire's newsroom where it was simultaneously transmitted to the city's major media points. Today, digital domains and social networks, websites, blogs, and mobile apps distribute news in algorithmic speed and analytical codes.

Social PR News Distribution Timeline and Highlights

Here's a brief overview of the history of PR news distribution:

- **1950s/1960s**: PR Newswire is the first to create a system to electronically deliver news releases to the New York media. Business Wire starts as a news release service.

- **1970s**: The first email is sent in 1971 and online forums emerged.

- **1980s**: AOL is launched, making the Internet more user-friendly. PR Newswire begins archiving news releases on electronic databases, including NEXIS (now LexisNexis (www.lexisnexis.com)).

- **1990s**: Internet Wire (now Marketwired (www.marketwired.com)) is launched as the first Internet-based press release distribution company. Business Wire is the first service of its type to put its clients' news online, launching the company's website, businesswire.com. PR Newswire is next to release news directly to consumers via the Web with the launch of prnewswire.com. Internet entrepreneur, David McInnis, starts PRWeb as a free online press release distribution service.

- **1999**: Blogger.com launched and was purchased by Google in 2003

- **2000–today**: In 2001, PR Newswire issues the first multimedia news release for Touchstone Pictures while promoting the film *Pearl Harbor*. PRWeb offers social bookmarking. Social media links are added to press releases. PR Newswire begins with del.icio.us and later adds Digg (digg.com), Reddit (reddit.com), Newsvine (newsvine.com), and StumbleUpon (stumbleupon.com). Business Wire starts adding social media tags to releases.

- **2003:** WordPress, a free and open-source blogging platforms, was launched. Today, WordPress is the most popular and largest blogging system in use on the Web with more than 60 million users.[5]

- **2008**: PitchEngine is founded by Jason Kintzler (www. jasonkintzler.com) as an alternative to the traditional press release and push distribution process of wire services and the first PR publishing platform.

- **2012**: Journalism gets sloppy and PR distribution services get a wake-up call. PRweb issues a fraudulent press release announcing Google's purchase of a Wi-Fi provider. The story is picked up by major media outlets, including AP, Reuters, The Next Web, USA Today, MSNBC, and TechCrunch.

- **2012**: Medium is introduced as a hybrid blogging and publishing platform founded by Twitter co-founders Evan Williams and Biz Stone.

- **2013**: Muck Rack lists thousands of journalists on Twitter, Facebook, Tumblr, Quora, Google+, LinkedIn and more who are vetted by a team of editors. Offers the one line press; added to Muck Rack's press release page and sent out by the @MuckRack (twitter.com/muckrack) Twitter account for $1 per character.

- **2014** LinkedIn introduces long form post publishing inside its network.

- **2015** Facebook introduces Instant Articles instantarticles. fb.com/

- **2015** Facebook reintroduces Facebook Notes

- **2016** Snapchat moves past Facebook in video views

---

[5]   en.wikipedia.org/wiki/WordPress

So Today: Storytelling and Publishing

Organizations have a host of choices when it comes to sharing and distributing company news. Brands are equipped with more publishing power than ever before and don't have to rely solely on third-party media outlets to post news. Now, they can do it automatically using their own newsroom, blog platform, social media networks, and also a variety of paid and free distribution and amplification services. Today's brands publish news through a blend of social media, search engines, brand advocates, mobile, visual, and traditional media.

News consumption continues its shift to search engines and social media. With that, social PR pros and content marketers double up as today's news editors and newsmakers by using publishing and distribution platforms beyond the press release.

For brands, publishing news to a paid wire service reaching traditional media and search engines is nothing new. But new outlets and platforms are bubbling to the top, offering savvy ways to reach and engage directly with your audience.

Social PR Press Release Distribution Tips

In the old-school days of PR, one press release could result in a wide variety of stories in different publications. As times change, new issues come up and the need for rich and fresh content presents a constant challenge.

Rather than push out the same version of a press release to all channels, repurposing one story into several fresh versions can help maximize distribution and avoid duplicate potential content issues from the stand point of the user and also the search engines. A brand's announcement can have the same message, optimized with the same keywords, but have a variety of different versions that can differ in headline, content intro, and the use of multimedia for best results. Get creative and give the same story a different twist.

The Social PR Distribution Checklist

- *Paid distribution version*: This could be a traditional 400-word news story optimized with strong visuals and video.

- *Website blog version*: This could be a longer version accompanied by an infographic that tells the visual story.

- *Social media version*: Using strong visuals with a call to action and short teasers of the story designed to lead the reader to the full story on the website newsroom or blog will help your company news stand out in the social news feed.

Today's Social PR Distribution Players

Packaging your company's news content for social media publishing and distribution is an effective way to reach your potential brand champions and create brand advocacy. Building rapport and relationships with consumers, businesses, and media who are most likely to not only choose your brand, but also advocate it to their friends, family, and coworkers, is key to social PR distribution. Social publishing allows you to increase reach and build trusted relationships and brand equity.

There's a win-win when it comes to press releases and content distribution: Press releases can be used to announce great content such as a how-to eBook or storytelling infographic, and press releases are also a form of newsworthy content.

Flowing and distributing your brand's news content through the various social news networks will ultimately generate the most visibility and leads.

Facebook

Your Facebook page is an extension of your business and can be an effective way to distribute company news and content while driving quality visits from Facebook (social media) to your website or blog (owned media). Using a strong visual, a short and optimized version of the news story with a link to the full story on your owned media is the first organic step that is free. As a brand with a Facebook page, you are in essence the editor of your company publication called *Your Facebook Page* and your Facebook Likes are the equivalent to your subscribers. Think of your Facebook page as a magazine and your company news content as part of the editorial strategy.

Reporting your company's news content in a Facebook-friendly way is the first step to driving quality visitors to your website or blog. You can also use Facebook's paid distribution with the Facebook Ad Manager or Power Editor to promote content along with to help your target audience see and engage with your news message, while also helping your target audience discover your news through their friends and targeted distributions. Explore targeting the media via workplace targeting and getting creative with your messaging and visuals in the newsfeed.

Facebook's most recent features such as custom audiences and website retargeting offer brands an effective way to build a quality social community based on the community you already have and the your recent website visitors.

Twitter

Twitter can be an effective way to reach the media and influential bloggers in your industry by using the social network as a means to find and follow story ideas and sources. A simple way to use Twitter is to organically broadcast your company news in an optimized fashion to your followers (and beyond) with hashtags and links back to full stories on your website or newsroom.

Promoted tweets take advantage of the paid side of Twitter, a social PR distribution option allowing you to put your company news in front of the right people by targeting by geography, gender, and interest. Paying to distribute news via Twitter can further amplify your message into the hands of the mobile market. You pay only when people click, favorite, reply, or retweet your news tweet.

Pinterest

It is possible to use Pinterest to tell your story without having to manage a Pinterest account. Be sure to create Pinterest friendly news content that come equipped with strong visuals. Make it Pin-worthy! Add some text overlays across images Include Pinterest's easy sharing options on your blogs such as the Save it button or create boards for your blog or your company newsroom to track media coverage. You can share the press room boards with the media. Pinterest reach is growing rapidly and is now more popular than Twitter with more than a fifth of American adults using the service, according to the Pew Research Center. Pinterest is an excellent way to go direct to your audience or let your audience spread the word for you in Pins and Boards. Pinterest ads were recently launched to small-to-medium sized businesses in early 2016. Pinterest offers a wide array of advertising tools, ranging from ads that advertisers can pay for depending on the engagement of the pin (from expanding the size of it all the way to clicking through and making a purchase) to its own spin on video advertisements that run a short clip as users scroll down on their feeds. (from techcrunch.com/2016/03/08/pinterest-opens-up-its-ads-manager-tools-to-smaller-and-medium-sized-businesses)

Instagram

If your customers are on Instagram, then you should be too! One of the best reasons to be on Instagram is because your customers are (and it's owned by Facebook.) In 2015, it opened up the advertising platform globally. Instagram's enhanced ad formats, targeting and buying options help advertisers drive the results they care about—from raising awareness to driving action. (business.instagram.com/advertising)

I love the example on the Instagram business blog about the yogurt-maker Chobani and how they use Instagram to connect with fans.

"We want to be where our consumers are," says Hilary duPont, Content Manager on Chobani's Brand Communications team.

"We're on the platform every day so we know what's trending. If our consumers are posting about smoothies, we are too. We want to be doing what they're doing."

Social PR Secret
Show a different side of your company by sharing inspirational pictures and reach a global audience in a very mobile and visual way.

Check out the official Instagram blog for more business idea and inspiration to use images and video to tell your story and connect with your audience.

P.S. Don't forget the hashtags!

LinkedIn

Share your news via the world's largest professional network, leveraging a blend of distributing LinkedIn Company Page, Employees, and Groups. Check out the paid side of LinkedIn by targeting journalists and bloggers in LinkedIn with a combination of general media-related job titles with industry-specific groups. LinkedIn is known as the professional social network and has "grown up" in a many ways over the past few years giving users and improved and robust visual and mobile opportunity.

What happens when you publish a long-form post on LinkedIn?

- Content: Your original content becomes part of your professional profile. It is displayed on the Posts section of your LinkedIn profile.

- Exposure: It is shared with your connections and followers.

- Distribution: Members not in your network can now follow you from your long-form post to receive updates when you publish next.

- Get found! Your long-form post is searchable both on and off of LinkedIn.

Google+

Launched in 2011, Google+ is Google's social side and should be taken into consideration as a news distribution option by combining the power of a Google+ Brand Page, Hangouts, YouTube, images, hashtags, and links back to full stories driving traffic back to your blog or website.

Remember that Google+ might not be the largest social network but it is owned by Google, the largest search engine. Your Google+ Page posts have the power to influence search results so be sure to optimize your content and update your Google+ Pages regularly for maximum Google love.

PitchEngine

Move over traditional distribution—PitchEngine empowers Social PR and marketing pros to create more sophisticated and visual content for consumers and journalists alike. The simple and easy-to-use software lets you package all of your brand or client's digital assets into a "pitch" and offers the capability to embed pitches, making the sharing of press releases and news easy and mobile-friendly. It also offers publishing perks like unlimited video, images, and sharing.

Triberr

Thanks to Triberr, I was able to get my SocialPRChat blog in front of an audience of journalists and bloggers from Forbes, Huffington Post, and countless influential bloggers who I can attribute much success in gaining exposure and visibility.

Triberr is a new and better way to grow your blog's readership. Why is it better? It connects like-minded bloggers and thought leaders we are interested in reading and supporting each other. If you have a blog with a news feed, try Triberr, a news content distribution and community building platform for bloggers.

Pay Distribution Services

Great content generates links and likes, and mediocre content will draw nothing but Panda penalties and no rankings.

Stick to higher-end distribution services that issue the press releases over a true newswire such as the following traditional PR distribution services that target the media, search, and include social services:

- Business Wire (www.businesswire.com)

- e-Releases (www.ereleases.com) (a personal favorite of mine for value, reach, and ROI)

- Marketwired (www.marketwire.com)

- PRWeb (www.prweb.com)

- PR Newswire (www.prnewswire.com)

Social PR Secret

Social PR hybrid news content distribution services under the radar include Triberr for news and industry bloggers and Haiku Deck for mobile and visual storytelling and presentations.

Content Promotion Tools Checklist

Know Your Audience Tools

Before your Social PR content can be created or promoted, it's pretty important to understand your target audience. Big data tools like Hitwise, Quantcast, Compete and Google's Keyword Planner let you to build out a Social PR promotion strategy by identifying where your audience spends their time online. In addition, tactical tools like Buzzsumo, Followerwonk, and Social Crawlytics can offer insight into what the trending and popular Social PR topics that are engaging and spiking consumer's interest online.

Paid to Play Social PR Promotion Tools

Paid Social PR content promotion can be effective for boosts in both driving traffic and engagement numbers. Leading content promotion networks like outbrain, Taboola, and Adblade intelligently distribute articles and videos across channels like CNN and time, displaying the content natively based on consumer behavior. Additionally, social media promotions on Facebook, Twitter, LinkedIn, Instagram, Pinterest, and YouTube.

The paid side of the social networks, the ones your audience is hanging out on, can be highly targeted and cost-effective, making these tools invaluable for ramping up Social PR engagement and improving ROI.

Earned Social PR Promotion Tools

It's all about relationship building, something carried over from traditional public relations best practices. Earned Social PR content promotion is about building mutually beneficial relationships to gain coverage from influencers in the online communities where your target audience is residing.

Major PR outreach software platforms like Cision, Vocus, Gorkana, and Meltwater provide assets like media databases and mass email capabilities that allow you to build lists of contacts and send pitches for editorial coverage. Tools such as HARO, Seek, or Shout and ProfNet are like the classified ads of the Social PR world.

By connecting news outlets with credible journalists and other resources, these tools help you make the most of your opportunities in specific verticals by providing access to subject matter experts.

Sources:

bit.ly/wfcFQI
bit.ly/RzfIX

Chapter 12
Live Streaming PR Secrets:
It's Your Story. Broadcast Now.

Smile. Start Broadcast. You're on the air!

J ust like that. Anyone with a smartphone has the power to broadcast live thanks to mobile streaming apps such as Twitter-owned Periscope, Snapchat, and Facebook Live.

If you've worked in the digital marketing world this past decade, you probably remember the buildup to "mobile is coming." It took much longer than anticipated for mobile to actually show up as a blip in the radar for marketers, but there's no doubt that mobile has arrived on the scene in a huge way starting in about 2013. Today, it's mobile or nothing with 60% saying they would not consider taking a vacation without their mobile device and, According to a Pew Research Center report, 46% of smartphone owners say that their smartphone is something "they couldn't live without."

While mobile was and is a big deal to everything search and social, it's nowhere near the explosive boom of video. With all eyes on mobile, video is the eye candy of choice, whether you're the producer or viewer. In 2016, 50% of video views are happening on mobile devices and the growth is projected to rise as video continues to be consumed by mobile users at a rapid rate.

Defining Live Video

Live video allows users to broadcast videos directly from their mobile devices to a variety of major social media platforms. It is a great way to promote a personal or corporate brand and increase engagement with key audiences.

The Live Video Players

Facebook Live: The best for last or better late than never. Facebook was a late bloomer to the live-streaming scene, launching Facebook Live to all users and Facebook Pages in March 2016. Predicted to be a game changer and stiff competition to Periscope, Blab, and the other players, Facebook Live makes it super simple to "go live" on your personal profile or Facebook Page. They made it available early to influencers such as Guy Kawasaki, who hosts Tech Tuesdays via Facebook Live where he gives quick tech tips to viewers.

Actors, athletes, journalists, and other public figures with verified profiles can go live from the Facebook Mentions app.

- Facebook Live is available on all personal profiles and pages.
- Users can edit videos on their timelines.
- Videos don't disappear after 24 hours, comments scroll, and users can embed them.
- Facebook altered its algorithm so live videos appear higher in users' news feeds.

Google HOA: Introduced in 2011 as a feature of Google+, Google HOA was one of the first platforms to make it easy for brands to broadcast live, on the air, and also be able to upload the video to YouTube for future broadcast. Hangouts On Air officially moved from Google+ to YouTube Live as of September 12, 2016.

Meerkat: First to market for livestreaming, Meerkat debuted at SXSW 2015 when it launched to the world with a big bang. Broadcasting live was born in a new social media fashion that's both raw and real. It handed over the coveted journalistic broadcast power to the mobile world. In March 2016, the company announced that it was leaving the live-streaming business to focus on building a video social network.

Periscope: Hatched just one month after Meerkat on March 26, 2015—and then quickly snatched up by Twitter—Periscope won the 2015 Apple App of the year award and quickly took the lead. Periscope lets you broadcast live video to the world from anywhere and instantly lets followers know they can can join, comment, or send you hearts in real time. The broadcast is available for replay for 24 hours or can be deleted any time after the broadcast. The more hearts you get, the higher they flutter on the screen. It even notifies your Twitter followers, goes live in your Twitter feed, and the video can be downloaded to your camera roll for other content uses.

- Twitter acquired the platform in January 2015 for $86.6 million
- In 2016, Periscope had more than 10 million users
- Live videos play directly on Twitter timelines
- Users can stream GoPro videos live via Periscope
- BMW, Experian, T-Mobile, Harley Davidson, and Central Park are brands using this well

Snapchat Live Stories: Launched in 2014, and orginally referred to as "Our Story," Snapchat Live Stories centers around an event, festival, concert, campus, sports match or a city-based story. Users submit their story and it's up to the Snapchat team to decide who gets picked to be part of the 24 hour "story." In February 2016, Snapchat caught up to Facebook with video views, which raised eyebrows with marketers, brands, and the industry.

YouTube Livestream and 360: You broadcast live from Google HOA direct to YouTube Live or create live-streaming video direct from your YouTube channel. Live streaming on YouTube is popular with gamers, YouTube stars, or soon-to-be YouTube stars use live streaming to interact with fans and build a following. YouTube account needed.

Blab: Launched in June 2015, Blab hit the live-streaming scene with the intention of bringing multiple people to the screen and live-streaming public conversations. Unfortunately, the party ended almost as quick as it started and the live streaming service called it quits in August 2016.

YouNow: Focused mostly on the millennial market, America's Got Talent holds auditions on it, and Huffington Post has a live show on the platform.

- The platform was founded in 2011
- It has 100-million user sessions per month and 150,000 active broadcasts per day
- BuzzFeed, Huffington Post, and Refinery29 are using it
- "America's Got Talent" holds live auditions on this platform
- YouNow has launched YouNow Latino, YouNow Deutsch and YouNow Arabic
- The broadcaster can monetize the video through virtual goods

What to watch for?

Video 360 and Virtual Reality are coming to the scene in a big way. "Livestreaming is the missing link between television and social media," Hackl predicts.

How Can Live Streaming Video Be Used in Social Media and PR?

From a PR perspective, live streaming videos is a publicist's dream. Here's why:

1. **Storytelling:** More than a Facebook post or a Tweet, live streaming gives us a huge opportunity for storytelling.

2. **Press Conferences:** Through the power of real-time video streaming, you no longer need the "press" to be present during press conferences. Game changer, right? The days of pestering media channels to broadcast your company's news are over. You have an added level of clarity with the messages you are trying to convey by being able to directly send that message to your intended audience. Bottom line: More control.

3. **Events:** Live streaming an event is a great way to engage a large audience. From live, behind-the-scenes footage to interviews with special guests to broadcasting the main attraction, there are many ways to capture an event to make your followers feel like they have VIP access. Your audience no longer has to be physically present; they just need to have an Internet connection. Make it fun, make it personal, and make it feel exclusive.

4. **Interviews:** Interviews with special guest or executives in real-time can enhance a company's transparency between its customers. Many times, interviews can appear staged and edited. With the use of Meerkat or Periscope, viewers are no longer speculating about the authenticity of an interview.

5. **Product Launches and Demonstrations:** This can apply to all types of companies. A product-based business can easily showcase its products using these apps and get valuable real-time feedback on their new items. A restaurant, for example, can show a cooking demonstration for a new dish. A real estate company can show houses to potential buyers. A clothing store can live stream a fashion show to lure in shoppers. The list goes on. This is also a useful platform to share promotions or deals.

6. **Breaking News and Responding to PR Disasters:** The beauty of live streaming is being able to respond immediately to breaking news or a PR crisis without relying on the media. If an issue needs to be clarified or addressed, an apology made, or even an influx of customer service issues on a new product, responding with live video is the most genuine approach.

7. **On-the-Spot How-To's:** Whether it's a quick tip on how to make your favorite drink or the ins and outs of writing your next best-selling book, now your followers can see you in action real-time.

8. **POVs:** While most agree the founding of the public relations profession started in 1900 with the launch of the Publicity Bureau, the POV (point of view) has been around for centuries as a means to brand and create thought leadership. Live streaming takes POV to a new level where perspectives and opinions are shared in real time and beyond.

9. **Talk Shows:** Creating your very own talk show has never been easier. Check out these YouTube shows for inspiration: #AskGaryVee, aimClear's Social Media Cluster Facts #SMCF, or Stone Temple's Here's Why.

10. **Coaching and Training:** Business, sports, fashion—you name it. Live streaming puts you and your brand center stage to share tips and educate a global audience with the push of a button.

11. **Discussions:** Discuss politics, world affairs, new books, interest rates, the economy, or even your favorite sports teams. Live video streaming increases the buzz factor for your favorite topic or event.

Examples of brands and organizations using live streaming:

- Huffington Post on Periscope
- Gary Vaynerchuk - Snapchat, YouTube, and Instgram
- Guy Kawasaki and Peter Shankman - Facebook Live
- Mari Smith - Facebook Live

Tips and Best Practices

I caught up with Cathy Hackl to share her Livestreaming PR Secrets with us. Here's what she shared and recommends for personal or business brands:

All of these different approaches to using these live-streaming video apps allow for a more personal relationship between the brand and its consumers.

Experiment: Know the basics of all the networks. Don't be scared to experiment with video. Social media and PR professionals will need know and master live streaming.

Equipment: We all have, for the most part, the same technology, but it's good to get a tripod to stabilize and a lavalier microphone for doing interviews. Inexpensive gear is now easier to get than ever before.

Wi-Fi: Having a good Wi-Fi connection is essential.

Standing Out: Naming your Periscope is important to attract live viewers. Capitalize the first letter of every word like a headline. Use emoticons and hashtags to optimize and stand out when the live stream is announced. Be forward about the name of the Periscope. Promote yourself via your other channels.

Frequency and Length: If you're holding a weekly show via live streaming, be consistent and reliable, Although the sweet spot is typically 15 minutes in length, if your topic is hot, then one hour or longer can definitely work.

Organize for Repurpose: Think ahead when creating live-streaming videos, especially when doing interviews, so that you can repurpose the interview content for future use. Hackl recommends taking questions at the beginning and end and letting live viewers know when they can ask questions so that live viewers know they will be able to ask questions.

Engaging Your Audience: It doesn't mean that you need to engage them every second, but to be successful, you must engage your audience during live streaming.

Block the Trolls: If you're doing live streaming for business, block the trolls right away and don't let them take away from the focus.

Measuring: It's easy to measure metrics straight from the app, metrics such as views, followers, and engagement.

12 Social PR Ways to Bolster Your Brand With Live Video by @CathyHackl

- Highlight breaking news or exclusive photos
- Demo and review products
- Interact with customer service
- Have an influencer take over the account
- Interview employees, customers, C-suite
- Share promotions or deals
- Attend conferences/panel discussions
- Tour retail spaces
- Connect with journalists and influencers
- Go behind the scenes
- Monitor competitors' strategies
- Respond to a PR crisis — C.H.

The Bottom Line

By using a live video platform, we are now able to significantly close the gap on the Know-Like-Trust (KLT) factor that we all aspire to within our respective communities. Strategically developed and implemented, live video can influence the decisions of your target audiences at a rate that you may not have seen with previous tactics. #GoLiveNow

Who to follow?
@CathyHackl
@KimGarst
@GaryVee
@GuyKawasaki
@GMScope - Global Meditation Scope
@Alroker
@Scobleizer

@Buzzfeed
@JimmyFallon

Notes

www.cision.com/us/2016/03/five-tips-on-using-live-streaming-video

www.prsa.org/Intelligence/Tactics/Articles/view/11455/1124/Now_Streaming_Live_Video_as_the_Latest_Tool_for_PR#.VyYtTKMrIkg

Chapter 13
Podcasting for Social PR: Listen up.

With the rise in mobile use, podcasts have made a comeback and are no longer just for the techie world. A podcast is similar to a radio program, but they are audio files typically listened to via sources such as iTunes. The word "podcast" originated from a blend of words "pod" (from iPod) and "broadcast."

Thanks to the iPhone and other smartphones, audio streaming is available at the touch of an app and can be accessed anytime and anywhere, including in your car, at your desk, at the beach, or working out.

Who is listening to podcasts? Studies show more than 20% of the 12–54 age group now regularly consumes on-demand audio programming and 23% of Millennials report regular listening to podcasts.

Thinking about starting your own Podcast? Go for it. From a public relations standpoint, it's the equivalent of hosting your own talk show and can boost credibility and authority in your industry.

I caught up with author, podcaster, and business coach Charlie Gilkey to get the inside scoop on the A,B,C's of podcasting and tapped into his Podcasting Social PR Secrets.

Podcast Realities

Between his business-coaching cocktails and book-writing wizardry, Charlie hosts The Creative Giant Show, a podcast that dives behind the scenes to talk about what it takes to thrive as a creative person who's actually making a difference in the world. It's a mix of interviews, jams, and riffs with Creative Giants at varying levels of success.

Podcast PR Secret #1

Think about search-friendliness for your podcast and episodes. People *search* iTunes for podcast topics, so consider what someone would be searching for when you're titling your podcast and episodes as if they were blog posts.

This works better for how-to and tips podcasts, but you can still use it for story-based or interview podcasts as well. If Seth Godin is on your podcast talking about marketing, then "3 Must-Apply Marketing Insights from Seth Godin" is significantly better than "Episode #21: Marketing Tips". The previous title is also much more social friendly.

Podcast PR Secret #2

Create a "home" page or a landing page on your website/blog for your podcast so that it's easy for people to find it without being in podcatchers and iTunes. Imagine that someone finds your podcast after you've recorded 50 episodes. How will they really know what the podcast is about? They get Episode 51 and have to figure it out from there. Or imagine that they want to share the podcast with their friends on Facebook, Twitter, or email (it happens!).

If you're not going to create a site specifically for your podcast, at least have a page on your website that introduces your podcast and makes it easy to share. As an example, check out the page for my podcast, The Creative Giant Show.

Podcast PR Secret #3

Create the podcast that you would want to listen to and that you'll enjoy producing. Data is all over the place about what works best for podcasts because it's such a versatile medium. Each host brings their own special sauce to it, and each community of listeners wants different things from their hosts. Some hosts can conduct a fascinating 45 to 55-minute interview that keeps people hanging on every minute, where others lose steam after 15 minutes. Some hosts can rock the 8-minute tip format, where others ramble and half-say something. Podcasting is a long game, so make sure that you enjoy it as you do it, or it's going to be a long grind. If you're not sure what you'll enjoy, just tell your listeners you're trying something new and do it.

Podcast PR Secret #4

Ask for reviews and tell people exactly how to do it on your FAQ page. Charlie Gilkey walks his audience through the steps using screenshots, a visual that actually shows people exactly how to do it. And don't be shy; ask for a five-star review. If you don't tell people what you want, they won't know what you want them to do. It's that simple. It only works almost every time.

Check out how Charlie does it on his FAQs Page: www.productiveflourishing.com/the-creative-giant-show/how-to-faq/

What's a podcast?

A podcast is like an audio blog. Rather than written content delivered to you via email or through a website, the audio episode goes right to your computer or mobile device. Podcasts are typically available as a series or have a theme.

How can I support a podcast?

Leaving a rating and review is the single best way to support the show. Next up would be sharing an episode with your friends or network.

Why is leaving a rating and review the best way to support the podcast?

In many ways, iTunes works like other search engines. iTunes uses ratings and reviews as a way to gauge popularity, and the more popular a podcast is, the higher it goes in its category's listing. But iTunes also uses the number of listens to determine how popular a show is, and the higher a listing the podcast is, the more listens it gets.

It creates a positive loop: The higher on the page a podcast is, the more listens it gets, and the more listens it gets, the higher on the page it goes.

Leaving a rating and review is something we can all do, whereas directly causing a bunch of listens is something only a few people do.

Listens, ratings, and reviews are important for three reasons:

1. They help us get great guests (if I don't already know them).

2. They affect the amount we can get from sponsors. It's expensive to run a great podcast, and we're far from breaking even in current expenses, let alone startup expenses.

3. They help us evaluate whether it's something we should keep doing. There are only so many things we can do,

and we're continually evaluating which projects are providing the most value to us and our community.

Leaving a rating is also a way for you to reciprocate in the value that you receive from the show, and it doesn't cost you anything. Thanks for your support!

What do you use to record your podcast?

My guests and I do a video meeting via Zoom, and I use a Hei-lPR40, Focusrite Scarlett 2i2, and my laptop. I upgraded to pro gear after I had done about 50 episodes.

By the way, though a lot of people use Skype, I found Zoom to be better because Skype recorded my guest and me at different volumes, and fixing it made the audio sound worse.

Another source is Zencastr.

How do you get big names on the podcast?

He says, "I'm blessed to personally know a lot of Big Names. Occasionally, I'll muster up the courage to ask some Big Name whom I don't know to be on the show. Sometimes they say yes. Then I freak out a little bit, count my blessings, and start prepping to make it the best interview they've had in a while."

Other ways might be to look at your LinkedIn connections, talk to conference speakers after a presentation or webinar, look for experts in your industry, or even check out posting on HARO (Help a Reporter Out) www.helpareporter.com. After all, you are now a journalist.

How do you figure out what to talk about?

For interviews, I mostly research what my guests are interested in, which makes me interested in it, too. I learn how they got to where they are and ask them to share that journey, especially the not-so-glamorous parts of it. I'm intensely curious about people. Though I always have questions to ask that my guests never see, I often abandon those questions. If I wanted canned conversations, I'd ask people to contribute something to the blog instead.

Solo riffs and jams with Angela are harder because I often can't see my own work. I try to pick content and ideas that are good brain food more than list-y stuff since list-y stuff works better as written content.

Who produces your podcast?

It's a team effort for The Creative Giant Show. The good people at Podfly handle the audio editing and get it into Libsyn for us. The rest of the workload is distributed among different members of the Productive Flourishing team. Shannon's the showrunner and manages guest coordination and chases me down, Macey works on the written content and promotional materials, and Vanessa designs the lead banners. Their support helps me focus just on the interviews and on recording great episodes.

Podcasting is a lot of work. How do you publish one episode, let alone two, per week?

Podcasting is a lot of work. A lot more than I estimated. But it's also something I really love doing, and it has business value for us, too.

The distributed workload above is the only way we get it done. As of mid-March of 2016, we're doing two episodes per week, and in case you're curious, publishing two times per week is more than twice as hard as publishing once per week. We might not continue doing it that frequently.

Ready to start a podcast? Make a plan but don't plan to be perfect.

Your show is calling!

Podcasts you might be interested in listening to for inspiration:

- The Social Media Examiner Show
- The Digital Dish hosted by Lisa Buyer and Cathy Hackl
- The Growth Show by Hubspot
- Copyblogger FM
- The Missing Link hosted by Jabez Lebret
- The Creative Giant hosted by Charlie Gilkey
- The #AskGaryVee Show

Looking for more? Check out this list of the top 50 Social PR geared podcasts for your listening pleasure with a little ROI. www.cision.com/us/2015/05/ top-50-pr-marketing-social-media-podcasters-to-follow/

Chapter 14
Mobile and Social PR Hook Up

Studies show the average American has his or her mobile phone within arm's reach 24 hours a day.[6] While mixing mobile phones with social media can definitely create a whole new set of crisis-based and reputation management PR services for a publicist or business owner, there's certainly an opportunity to use mobile as a means to deliver news and create positive and proactive publicity for an organization or personal brand.

In the summer of 2012, I started noticing these very inspiring messages popping up on my Instagram feed, all of which were branded with the same black background with a white typewriter style font and all of which were thought-provoking bits of life and business wisdom. The messages were streaming from Sarah Evans' newsfeed and were also being shared on her Facebook page. After about 30 days of mystery messages, the story broke: Sarah was launching a book titled, *[RE]FRAME: Little Inspirations for a Larger Purpose* (amzn.to/1wxtyUH). Evans describes *[RE]FRAME* as one part personal journey and one part prescriptive steps to help people reconnect to their purpose.

---

6   Morgan Stanley

Mobile PR: She Moves in Mysterious Ways

Inspired by Sarah's book launch, here are a few ideas for using mobile for social PR that can be used to cinch some publicity for another product or service launch:

- Use a combination of visual, mobile, and social as a testing ground before a campaign launch. This mini focus group can quickly give insight as to what resonates with your brand followers and what doesn't. Testing various images, scenes, topics, and more can be extremely valuable and resourceful before launching any product, service, or even content.

- Teasing images and mysterious messaging can get people intrigued as to what it is all leading up to, similar to what movie teasers are designed to do.

- Enroll your audience and create a relationship with them on a topic before you really have something to sell.

- Make sure analytics are in place to measure, assess, and take action. Sarah used SimplyMeasured and WEBSTA *formerly known as Webstagram* in her visual and social PR campaign.

Sarah tested out a variety of different messages before her book launched. She measured which ones scored in the analytics, and only the top ones made the cut for her book. Thanks to social media you can test out messaging before spending a ton of time and resources in printing and publishing.

The Rise of Mobile: It's Here

Mobile is everything. Mobile is mandatory. Taking your company news and publicity mobile isn't on the social PR *maybe* list—it's on the *must* list. In fact, it's on the everyday to-do list. Ask yourself, "How can this message get to the mobile user?"

Consider the following when it comes to how mobile is changing our lives and the face of PR:

According to a Pew Research Center report, 46% of smartphone owners say their smartphone is something "they couldn't live without," compared to 54% who say their phone is "not always needed." April 2015 4

Consumers are not going on desktop to share brand messages, rather they are going to mobile devices. Flurry's most recent study shows 86% of mobile usage is within apps. April 2014

- Nine out of 10 mobile searches lead to action and over half lead to purchase, according to a Search Engine Land article (selnd.com/1ut6ZlJ).

- 70% say they use mobile technologies to follow or monitor news and information. 41.7% say they frequently and 9.2% say they always share or recommend news from their mobile device, according to a TEKGROUP International.

Mobile PR 101: Ways to Get Good (or Bad) PR

- *A mobile-friendly website or blog is good Social PR*: If this is not happening yet, you're on your way to become indexed with this hashtag: #FAIL. Have you looked at your brand's website or blog on a mobile device? If it's not mobile-friendly, you could be losing mobile visitors at "hello." Make sure the website or blog loads quickly, is easy to navigate, and offers quick, on-the-spot access to business information such as directions, contact information, and how to easily make a purchase.

- *Let customers find you in Google no matter what device they are using. Get up to speed using Google My Business.* (google.com/business)

- *Read all about it via a mobile-friendly online newsroom*: Make it easy for the media, influencers, bloggers, and customers to learn about your latest news via mobile, especially since 77% say they visit corporate news websites or online newsrooms using their mobile devices.

- *Think of the mobile user when communication via social media.* If you don't have a mobile-friendly website, at least make sure your social media networks are making up for it. Be sure your cover images and profile images work all across all mobile devices. Do an audit – go check out what your brand's social media accounts look like on different mobile devices, including your blog. Is anything broken? Think of the user experience first.

"It is amazing how many brands are not taking geo-location seriously, especially considering the mobile search opportunity," said SEO expert and Pubcon Speaker Liaison Joe Laratro (bit.ly/1q8PG2D) in a Search Engine Watch interview (bit.ly/1ywFoxR).

Laratro offers these mobile PR mistakes to avoid for brands looking to gain mobile search visibility:

- The company's contact information is on the home page but is part of an image, instead of HTML.

- Not including a physical address in the footer and not using schema markup.

- Not writing the content of the website in a geo-centric manner.

- Not claiming and regularly monitoring your Google+ local/business listing.

Check out your Google Analytics page. See what the mobile traffic looks like and how it is growing. Is your brand ready?

Social PR Secret

Make your blog mobile-friendly in minutes! If you want a fast and easy way to build a great-looking mobile website quickly, check out DudaMobile (www.dudamobile.com).

Chapter 15
The Rise of Visual Reporting

Heard it through the social PR Vine, Snap, or an Instagram video news report? That's how brands can break news in today's visual PR world.

"Brands that can rock in visual media will find themselves market leaders," was the closing line of a popular and timely *Fast Company* article by Ekaterina Walter (twitter.com/ekaterina), Intel's former social media strategist and author of *The Wall Street Journal* bestseller, *Think Like Zuck: The Five Business Secrets of Facebook's Improbably Brilliant CEO Mark Zuckerberg* (amzn. to/1uPBSy5).

Using strong visuals to tell, sell, and share a story is nothing new. After all, even Traditional Journalism 101 relied on the cover image to sell a newspaper or magazine on the newsstands. Today's cover stories don't just happen by journalists. Instead, visual stories are part of the daily social newsfeed. In PR, offering strong visuals with a press release always seemed to help get your press release to stand out on the editor's desk, but now everyone is a potential editor.

If you think press releases are dead, yours might be because they don't include any visuals. Go check out your past press releases in your newsroom or online. Chances are they didn't include any visuals with the distribution. Imagine posting something on Facebook without a visual; that's almost a misdemeanor!

The Dawn of Visuals Means the Rise of Press Releases

A recent PR Newswire analysis of its press release data revealed that press releases using multimedia assets garner significantly more visibility (bit.ly/1q8PUa5) than text-only releases—up to 9.7 times more.

Social PR Secret
Adding a strong photo, video, and/or a downloadable file to a press release distribution can increase your online visibility by 10 times the views.

Text was then, but visuals are now:

- 44% of users (and journalists) say they are more likely to engage with your brand's news posts if the story includes pictures than any other updates. (ROI Research) *That's good PR!*

- 60% of consumers are more likely to consider or contact a business if their images appear in local search results. (Bright Local) *That's good PR!*

- A 37% increase in engagement occurs when Facebook posts include photographs. *That's good PR!*

- 79% of journalists report that images increase the odds of a press release getting picked up. (TEKGROUP) *That's good PR!*

- Readers are four times more likely to engage or comment on a blog post with a good image. *That's good PR!*

- 94% more total views on average are attracted by content containing compelling images than content without images. *That's good PR!*

- 67% of consumers consider clear, detailed images to be very important and carry even more weight than the product information, full description, and customer ratings. *That's good PR!*

Today's company news can happen with a picture, a video, a GIF, or a Pin and it's social, optimized and, above all, visual.

Social PR Secret
Check out Twitter Cards to add visual impact from your content to Twitter.

Infographic Storytelling Insights

"The best infographics convey a lot of information in a lot less space than it would take to write about the topic or have regular graphs of the data." According to Mike Volpe (www.linkedin.com/in/mikevolpe), past CMO at HubSpot, a marketing software company.

Emojis Prove to Rock Social PR Messaging ☺

Is it possible for an emoji to tell your Social PR story? Survey says: Yes! Even though it may be a small part of your messaging, emojis are visual and make a big difference when it comes to engagement. Posts and social messaging that use emojis receive 52% more Facebook fan engagement! These posts have a 57% higher like rate, 33% higher comment rate and 33% higher share rate. Facebook emoticons help humanize your brand's message and increase fan engagement. Say it with a smile! ☺ [7]

---

[7]   Buddy Media and www.bitrebels.com/social/facebook-science-engagement-infographic

Tools and Apps to Make Your Social PR Life Easier

We talked about the critical nature of the use strong visuals and the all-encompassing mobile news opportunity, but this doesn't mean you need to add a team of commercial artists to your roster. It would be a nice luxury, but beside the cost, you don't have the time. Here are some super easy tactics that won't break the bank, but can be highly effective in the mobile market.

- Canva: (www.canva.com) Amazingly simple graphic design for social messaging and blogs.

- PicMonkey (www.picmonkey.com): You don't have to be a Photoshop pro to make great photo edits. Make collages, edit, and have access to a hoard of great effects, supreme fonts, overlays and more!

- InstaQuote (bit.ly/VmqTiX): Use this Social PR Secret to add text to images for social network messaging, blog posts, and press releases to make quotes and stats stand out in the newsfeed.

- 123rf (www.123rf.com): Find the perfect image for your campaign without having to stage it yourself. These royalty free stock photos offer a great library of images for purchase so you don't have to worry about copyright infringement.

- Piktochart (piktochart.com): This great app for infographic production allows brands to tell their story in a beautiful and easy-to-share way. Choose a theme and enjoy the freedom to edit everything and anything.

- Infogr.am: Another great tool for making infographics, but this one is interactive! Edit data through the built-in spreadsheet and see the results immediately.

- Visual.ly: Need some awesome videos, infographics or presentations but don't have an in-house creative team? Get connected with a handpicked team to help you achieve your creative goals for your campaign.

- Camera+ (bit.ly/1pOfHXL): By far the best photo editing in my book. With more than 10 million downloads at the time of this writing, Camera+ is my go-to photo editing app that delivers brilliance in editing, cropping, and color retouching.

- Haiku Deck (www.haikudeck.com): This free presentation app is designed to make your Social PR life easier. Whether you are pitching the media a story, presenting at a conference, or putting together a presentation for new business or product launch, HaikuDeck will set your visual world free! Once I met HaikuDeck, I broke up with PowerPoint—and you will too!

- Instagram (instagram.com): The latest updates go beyond filters. Adjust contrast, saturation, brightness and more without having to edit on a desktop.

- Vine (www.vine.com): This could be your answer to short pitches, getting attention, or sliding in some humor to your company news in 6 seconds or less of video power.

Visual PR Skills Snapshots

- Create original images by customizing stock photography with headlines.

- Curate a library of images using Instagram or similar filters and creative cropping.

- Optimize images and videos for search and social with keyword-rich file names, titles, descriptions, and alt tags.

- Learn some simple mobile photography skills, such as lighting, composition, and editing.

- Create typography-based images with inspirational quotes or statistics.

- Use interesting and evoking images with blog posts and press releases. Make it Pin-worthy!

- When launching a new product, do not just have the "hero" shot, take photos of the product in use or in application.

- Take a Pinterest baby step: Create a board on Pinterest for blog posts and media coverage.

- Get inspired from other successful brands using visual social media to share, report, and tell their story.

- Optimize your images when using them with blogs and website content to take advantage of Google image search results.

- Borrowing an image? Keep it legal. Get permission first, and make sure you provide a photo credit with a link back. Also, watermark images with your logo to prevent image hijacking.

- Evaluate your online newsroom and make visuals part of your social PR content strategy.

- Don't be afraid to #fail! Try #newthings and #win with #VSMM (Visual Social Media Marketing)!

Social PR Secret

An excellent infographic is one that not only makes readers say, "This is awesome," it makes them say, "This is awesome—and now I'm gonna share it with everyone I know!"
—Jesse Thomas, founder of Jess3

Sources:
bit.ly/Rj0OIv
slidesha.re/bgr0uc
slidesha.re/ML9fNe
bit.ly/14uU4hc
bit.ly/JOSyxu

Chapter 16
Visual PR Secrets
89 Free Graphic and Image Sources

It's no secret; images are the key to grabbing the attention of your audience. But in today's social streaming eye candy world, stock images just won't do the trick. We must think and act as a creative director, even if you have to fake it to make it. So thanks to some incredible researchers who want to help us think outside the stock image box, we've curated this list to help you find that perfect image source.

1. 123RF

123RF is a popular, royalty-free resource that offers millions of images, audio, videos, and vectors for a fee. Note: 123RF also has a huge library of free images available to its members (membership is free). The free images are very small and require attribution.

2. 500px

500px allows you to search for Creative Commons-licensed photos, a popular photo community with impressive high-quality images. No membership required, but not all images on 500px are free to use.

3. Adobe Post App

Create stunning graphics in seconds for free! Get started in seconds with professionally designed, eye-catching templates that you can tweak in simple steps.

4. Albumarium

Albumarium is a stock library featuring images for personal and commercial use covering a number of categories like nature, animals, and buildings. Check copyright privileges before use.

5. Ancestry Images

Free image library of historical prints. Inquire directly if you'd like to use the images commercially.

6. BeFunky

BeFunky is a design tool that is easy enough to use that anyone can create beautiful photographs and professional-quality graphic design without any special skills or technical expertise.

7. DesignersPics

Photos found on DesignersPics are given copyright-free by photographer, web designer, and developer, Jeshu John. Attribution is requested but not required.

8. BigPhoto

BigPhoto offers you free downloads of all the pictures in our massive and constantly growing photo gallery. You can use these images as you wish for personal or commercial purposes (see copyright for details).

9. Canva

An online, graphic design platform. It offers free access to a wide assortment of design tools and options, as well as premium options for paying customers.

10. Compfight

Compfight is an image search engine tailored for efficiently locating images for blogs, comps, inspiration, and research.

11. CreativeCommons.Photo

Search high-quality free images with Creative Commons Zero CC0 licenses.

12. Cupcake

All photos on Cupcake are licensed under the Creative Commons license CC0, which means that you are free to use the images without any costs.

13. Death to the Stock Photo

Death to the Stock is a photo and inspiration haven for creatives crushing their path. Free photos by mail every month. Sign up today!

14. Dreamstime

Dreamstime not only offers a huge collection of royalty free stock, but they also offer absolutely free stock photos for the price of attribution.

15. Easel.ly

Easel.ly is a simple web tool that empowers anyone to create and share powerful visuals—no design experience needed!

16. Easy Cover Maker

Free tool to create social media covers with some free templates.

17. Epicantus

Free original photography by Daria. You can contact her for questions here: www.bydaria.com/#contact

18. Every Stock Photo

Everystockphoto.com is a license-specific photo search engine. Currently, they index and search millions of freely licensed photos from many sources and present them in an integrated search.

19. FindA.Photo

Search through thousands of free (CC0-licensed) stock photos by color with FindA.Photo.

20. Foodies Feed

Foodies Feed stock repository is filled with yummy images of great food taken by photographer Jakub Kapusnak. Attribution isn't required.

21. Foter

Foter hosts more than 220 million free Creative Commons images. These images are from numerous online sources (Foter uses the Flickr API and searches Creative Commons photos). What makes Foter unique is their WordPress plugin.

22. FreeDigitalPhotos.net

FreeDigitalPhotos.net has free, small-sized photos (if you want larger files, you have to pay) that can be used for personal or commercial use. There are tens of thousands of images on the site

23. FreeImages.com

FreeImages.com hosts more than 387,000 free photos and illustrations. Be sure to read the Content License Agreement and also view specific restrictions for each image, which can be seen on the preview screen.

24. Free Media Goo

Free Media Goo provides a way for developers to gather royalty-free photography that can be used in print, film, TV, Internet, or any other type of media for both commercial and personal use.

25. Free Nature Stock

Free Nature Stock provides royalty-free nature stock photos. Use them however you want. Created by Adrian Pelletier. Updated daily.

26. Free Range Stock

Free Range Stock was formed with the goal to provide quality stock photos for commercial and non-commercial use. For free.

27. Free Stock Image Point

Free Stock Image Point has no copyright restrictions (CC0 1.0 Universel).

28. FreeImages.Pictures

FreeImages.Pictures is a repository for Flickr, Wikimedia, Pixabay, morgueFile, Openclipart, and Google Custom Search.

29. Free Photos Bank

FreePhotosBank offers a searchable database of free to use stock images.

30. GetRefe

GetRefe is a royalty-free, high-quality, real life collection of photos.

31. GIPHY GIF Maker

GIPHY GIF Maker allows you to create animated GIFs from video files and YouTube links.

32. Gratisography

Gratisography showcases free photos by Ryan McGuire that are offered under the same terms as Creative Commons Zero. As the photographer puts it, there are some common sense limitations to using the photos, but attribution isn't required.

33. Good Free Photos

Good Free Photos is a large, free stock photo site with thousands of public domain photos including landscapes, objects, animals, plants, textures, and many other free photos.

34. Haiku Deck

Haiku Deck is the easiest way to create an amazing presentation on the web, iPad, or iPhone. Embed and save as your Haiku deck as a video, and then you can repurpose it on YouTube, Facebook, Twitter, or any other digital asset you own.

35. IM Free

IM Free offers thousands of high-resolution images in various collections. You can use the search box to find what you're looking for or browse the collections. Note: attribution to the creator is required.

36. Image Finder

Image Finder crawls and displays images licensed under Creative Commons from various stock image sites.

37. Info.gram

Info.gram is a free tool to create infographics and interactive online charts. It's free and super easy!

38. ISO Republic

ISO Republic offers free and premium high-quality photos for creatives. Images are from photographer Tom Eversley.

39. Jay Mantri

JayMantri provides free, gorgeous images that can be used under Creative Commons Zero.

40. JÉSHOOTS

JÉSHOOTS images are free of copyrights under the Creative Commons public domain deed CC0.

41. Kaboompics

Kaboompics offers free hi-res images daily. Use the Search Box, click #Tag under the photo or choose Category to see images you are looking for. Attribution required.

42. Life of Pix

Life of Pix offers free High-Resolution Photos, no Copyrights Restrictions. On a side note, if you need videos, check out Life of Vids.

43. Little Visuals

Little Visuals offers seven free images sent every seven days to your inbox. Sign up required (it's free!).

44. LogoGarden

Logo Garden custom logo design is a free online logo maker and generator.

45. Magdeleine

Hand-picked free photos for your inspiration. Search easily by keyword, color, category, or license.

46. MMT.li

MMT.li offers free for commercial use (CC0) photos by @jeffreybetts. Use them in your projects and any way you want. Follow for new photos each week.

47. Morguefile

Morguefile offers free stock photo archive for creatives by creatives. If you are planning to use the image for personal or commercial use, it is recommended that you get in contact with the photographer and include a byline with the image that includes the photographer's name.

48. Moveast

Moveast features photography of the Eastern world that is free to use.

49. New Old Stock

New Old Stock offers free vintage photos from the public archives. Free of known copyright restrictions.

50. New York Public Library

The New York Public Library has Digital Collections with over 180,000 items that are in the public domain and are available as high-resolution downloads.

51. Pagemodo

Make a Facebook Cover photo for free. Pagemodo gives you access to thousands of free stock images and shapes and the ability to upload your own images.

52. Profile Picture Maker

Profile Picture Maker's site is equipped to help you create great photos for Facebook, Twitter, LinkedIn, Google+, and more.

53. Pexels

Pexels pictures are free for personal and even for commercial use, meaning the pictures are completely free to be used for any legal purpose.

54. Photos Everywhere

Photos Everywhere is a collection of high-resolution travel stock images. There are over 3,600 photos that are free to use and ready for instant download.

55. PhotoPin

PhotoPin is one of the easiest ways to search Flickr. PhotoPin allows you to search by commercial or non-commercial license and download the images without leaving the site.

56. Photober

Photober offers free images; however, you need to attribute credit to Photober.

57. PicJumbo

PicJumbo offers a huge collection of high-resolution images for personal and commercial use and does require attribution.

58. PickUp Image

Pickupimage is a large collection of free photographs. Free download high-quality premium, free stock images and public domain photos.

59. PicMonkey

PicMonkey is a free, online photo editor and collage maker. It offers basic editing all the way up to advanced stuff like touch-up and cloning.

60. Picography

Picography offers free hi-res photos. Use them however you'd like.

61. Piktochart

Piktochart is an easy infographic design app that requires very little effort to produce beautiful, high-quality graphics. You can start out for free and make your own infographics.

62. Pixabay

Pixabay has over half a million illustrations, and vectors. As stated on their website, all images are released under Creative Commons CCO into the public domain and can be used royalty-free, including for commercial purposes. Attribution is not required.

63. Pixlr

Pixlr is a free, online image editor. Enables to fix, adjust, and filter images in a browser.

64. Public Domain Archive

Everything you need for your creative projects, all public domain images.

65. Raumrout

Raumrout has hand-picked and high-resolution quality photos available online. The gallery is small but good.

66. re:Splashed

re:Splashed has free HD images for your web and design projects.

67. Recite This

Recite This has a ton of different design themes that will easily make your quote look great. Just plug your quote into the box they provide and choose a template for free.

68. RGB Stock

RGB Stock has more than 100,000 free stock photos.

69. Skitterphoto

Skitterphoto has added a new image every day since its inception in 2014 with access to unique high-resolution photos. The images are taken by three photographers and are available under the Creative Commons Zero license.

70. Smithsonian on Flickr

Smithsonian Institute on Flickr has many images under public domain usage for you to download for free without attribution or other restriction.

71. Snapographic

Snapographic is a collection of high-res photos by photographer Thomas Mühl. Attribution is not required.

72. Snapwire Snaps

Snapwire Snaps gives seven free photos every seven days. License and commission photos from some of the world's most talented photographers.

73. Splashbase

Splashbase allows you to search several stock libraries such as unsplash, Life of Pix, Jay Mantri and more.

74. Splitshire

Splitshire is an instant-download high quality free stock photos without copyright, do whatever you want. Daily updates!

75. Startup Stock Photos

Startup Stock Photos has free photos for startups, bloggers, publishers, websites, designers, developers, creators, and everyone else.

76. Stockpholio

Stockpholio is an easy-to-use photo search site that offers varying collection of Creative Commons licensed images from Flickr.

77. StockPhotos.io

StockPhotos.io is a sharing community that has a collection of many free photos. According to StockPhotos.io, "only public domain or Creative Commons licensed photos that are allowed for commercial use are added on this site." Make sure to check the licensing of each photo to avoid legal issues.

78. StockSnap.io

StockSnap.io is a site that offers hundreds of high-resolution photos. According to the curator, each of their images is released under Creative Commons Zero and can be copied, modified and distributed, including images that will be used commercially. No attribution is required.

79. Stockvault

Stockvault offers over 75,000 free photos, textures, and art illustrations.

80. Stokpic

Stokpic offers free stock photos for commercial use. (Stokpic License) allows you to do anything apart from redistribute.

81. Superfamous

Superfamous features beautiful eye-catching photographs by Folkert Gorter. They can be used for your own purposes, as long as you give credit.

82. Travel Coffee Book

Travel Coffee Book is an effective site if you are looking for landmarks and scenery photos. All images are available under Creative Commons Zero.

83. Unrestricted Stock

Unrestrictedstock.com offers royalty-free images, videos, and vectors at no cost. As stated on their website, you can do pretty much anything with their online collections. The license agreement only has a few restrictions, which should be checked out before using their stock.

84. Unsplash

Unsplash is a free photo website that offers ten new high-resolution photos added every ten days and all images are licensed under Creative Commons Zero. SocialPRSecret There is an Unsplash Instant plugin for Chrome.

85. UPICM

UPICM "free pics, no tricks." No attribution is required and the image library is filled with many images you won't find elsewhere. UPICM also offers stock images for a fee and/or a buyout option.

86. Visual.ly

Visual.ly's free data visualization tools allow you to create infographics in seconds. Try it out and start generating your own custom infographics.

87. Wikipedia Commons

Wikimedia Commons offers creative common and public domain images. Check to see if attribution is required.

88. WordSwag App

WordSwag is a great app with cool fonts, typography generator, creative quotes, and text over pic editor!

89. Wylio

Wylio is an easy to use Creative Commons image finder. Wylio uses the Flickr API to populate its search returns. Membership is required but free for basic search and functionality.

Social PR Secret

Know when and when not to design. Remember, being efficient in the Social PR world is important to your success. Know when to get help from services like Fiverr when you are on deadline.

Social PR Secret

Know your image-to-word ratio. According to research by @BuzzSumo, articles with an image every 75 to 100 words get the most shares. But don't go crazy, just use this as a guideline to make sure you stay focused on word count and images.

Social PR Secret

Avoid the most used and common stock images. The last thing you need is for your competition to use the same image as you in their social media or blog posts.

Social PR Secret

Make it memorable. Edit, crop, filter, saturate, lens, sticker, doodle, and overlay. One of my favorite tools is Canva, but the most important thing is to choose or create stand out images that are memorable. After editing, you can use the MIT memorability tool memorability.csail.mit. edu/demo.html to find how well the image will stick with readers.

Contributing Sources: Mindy Weinstein/SEJ and Canva

Scientific Reasons People Are Wired to Respond to Your Visual PR

Your brain allows you to interact with the world, learn, grow, and understand. It can do a lot of amazing things, and it wants to do so through your eyes. Brains are made for looking, and if your brand is not taking advantage of the brain's constant hunger for new visual information, then it's missing out on one of the best ways to tap straight into people's' heads.

Below are 10 scientific reasons people are wired to respond to your visual public relations and marketing.

Visual processing is what our brains were made for

Your brain is really one big organ trying to make sense of the world, and it does that almost entirely through vision. Of course, we also smell, taste, touch, hear and such (we actually have way more than five senses, perhaps up to 21) but seeing is our primary sense, by a long distance.

Color captures attention…

Color is one of the best tools visual marketing has at its disposal. Adding color to documents such as safety notices and warnings has been shown to increase recall of that technical information by up to 82%.

But why? Why are we automatically attracted to some colors, and reject others? A 2009 study from Berkeley, California looked at why we associate certain colors with good and certain colors with bad, and it comes down to what those colors represent, and our own personal preferences. Because blues and greens are associated in nature with good health and cleanliness, they have come to mean that for us still. That is why advertisers often use blues and whites to illustrate freshness and clean living.

The bottom line is that if you want to play safe, always pick blue. And if you want to play dangerous, always pick red.

...as does movement.

The eye is made up of cones and rods. Cones are good for detail and for color; while rods cannot detect color, they detect movement and allow for vision in low-level light.

We are watching from Day 1

When a baby is born their visual system is not completely ready; yet, it is soon stormed by thousands of new sights, and it learns quickly what to pay attention to. Babies, first learn to focus on individual objects and begin to learn that certain shapes are associated with objects. This is one of the reasons that visuals are so appealing to humans. We inherently understand visual metaphors because we have learned to associate objects with behaviors from such an early age, far before we learned how to describe those objects or behaviors in words.

We are hard-wired to respond to faces

When we are born, one of the first things we focus on are faces. The reason being that the brain has a specific circuit for recognizing faces called the fusiform gyrus, or the fusiform face area.

Our brains love to be stimulated

The brain is extremely good at filtering constant information. It is constantly being bombarded with new information every second— just sit now and think of all of the sights, smells, touches, etc. that you are receiving. The brain has to act as the gatekeeper to the conscious mind, throwing out everything that isn't needed at this very second. If you hear a piece of information, then a few days later you will only remember 10%, however, if you add a picture to that information, recall goes up to 65%. This is because adding visuals to a written piece can help keep the brain entertained, attending, and interested.

Our brains love simplicity

Less is always more. As much as our brains need stimulation, they respond to simplicity. Visuals are a great way of reducing information to simple ideas. It may be a cliché, but it is also true: a picture speaks a thousand words.

You can add emotion

The best way to get people involved with a brand is through personal connections and personal stories. If an imagine speaks a thousand words, then an emotion speaks a million. Of course, expressing emotion through words is possible, but humans are masters at reading people's facial expressions and are always on the lookout for emotional cues. Thus, associating your brand with positive emotions is a great way to connect with the public.

We can understand visual information in an instant

An MIT study suggest that we can understand the meaning of an image in about 13ms, that is ten times faster than the blink of an eye! Therefore, if you want to get an idea or a point across, then an image is by far the best way to do it.

We remember visually

Close your eyes and try to remember something, a picture will instantly come to mind it's inevitable. Not only do we remember visually, we remember visuals far better than words. We are able to remember up 2,000 pictures with only a little learning and recognize them days later!

Words just don't cut it anymore, if you want your brand to stand out and be remembered, visuals are a must. By including visuals in your marketing, you will allow people to understand in an instant, what your brand is about and what you want to say.

Article Credit: This article originally appeared on Canva and was written by Andrew Tate. The full article can be read at designschool.canva.com/blog/visual-marketing/

Social PR Secret

Download Canva's iPhone app! You get all the tools, layouts and magic Canva offers on a smaller screen, while keeping the experience simple.

Carry your designs with you and edit them on the go, create new designs with 100's of layouts professionally designed for the iPhone and switch seamlessly between your devices. What more can you ask for?

Chapter 17
Scoring Influence

Social PR and influence are like cookies and cream: they go together. By putting them together, you can have a slam dunk in publicity and credibility. To a certain degree, scores do matter when it comes to a brand's credibility, visibility, and expertise positioning.

Klout (www.klout.com) and Kred (www.kred.com) are among today's most popular social influence reporters. In the real-time world of social integration, authenticity, engagement, and influence do matter and the data is publicly displayed. The question, however, is this: *How much does it matter, and who should really care?* Organizations, brands, the media, and individuals are getting scored, ranked, and labeled on influence.

How Klout Works

The Klout Score measures influence based on your ability to drive action. Every time you or your brand create content or engage, you influence others. The Klout Score uses data from social networks in order to measure:

- *Activity*: The frequency of your social posts and the social actions you take on other people's content.

- *True Reach*: How many people you influence.
- *Amplification*: How much you influence them.
- *Network Impact*: The influence of your network.
- *Content*: Any media that you post to social networks.

How Kred Works

Kred measures influence and outreach in all of your online communities in real time and is completely transparent in its scoring system, unlike Klout.

The Kred Score uses data from social networks in order to measure:

- *Activity*: "Generous" actions like engaging with others and spreading their message (re-tweeting or re-sharing).
- *True Reach*: How many people you influence.
- *Network Influence*: You get more points if someone with a large following does something for you.
- *Engagement*: The ability to inspire action from others like re-tweets, replies, or new follows.
- *Network Impact*: The influence of your network.
- *Content*: Kred's Community Scores are based on "Influence and Activity" with other people that Kred has assigned to that community.

Ego Power or Social PR Strategy?

Internet marketing experts say brands should pay attention to scoring systems such as Klout and individuals should forget about them. For the social PR professional, that means your brand's social influence score could be a means of evaluating expertise on certain subject. A higher score of influence could be more influential to a reporter, a mark of a clean and credible reputation, and the difference of winning an important media or new business interview opportunity.

Moving Content Through an Engaged Network

Whether Klout, Kred, or other influential players such as PeerIndex (now a part of Brandwatch), or the offline world, building a social network that delivers a strong ROI has some common foundational elements.

How to Increase Your Social Score on Klout and Kred: The Basics

- Build a relevant network.

- Have a compelling content sharing strategy.

- Systematically engage influencers who can push your content virally.

Klout Score Influencers

- Twitter and Facebook carry the most weight.

- LinkedIn and Foursquare don't seem to pull much rank.

- Google+ matters.

- There's some correlation between number of +K's earned and high Klout scores.

- Bing and Instagram are now factored into its social influence measurement tool.

What Can You Do Right Now?

- Check your social score on both influence tools.

- Scope out your competitors' social score and use this as a competitive analysis opportunity.

- Make sure Klout or Kred topics accurately portray your brand profile, persona, and expertise influences.

- See how Klout or Kred can fit into your social PR business model. If it makes sense, spend more time with a strategy. If it's not a fit, don't waste time worrying about it.

- Try it out for 30 days and see what happens.

- Use these social scores as a means to benchmark if you are trying to monitor improvement or gain competitive insight.

- Use social scores and measurement as a means to research brands and individuals. You can see at a glance what a reporter is engaging in, sharing, and interacting with.

- Don't obsess over it.

How to Improve Your Social PR Influence Score

- Stay active on your social channels publishing content five to seven days a week. Reminder: social media is more than a full-time job.

- Keep visibility on your social sites steady and flowing on a daily basis.

- Stay on top of the favored social network. This seems to be a moving target and brands need to move with it.

- Interact with other influencers.

- Post engaging and electrifying photos with visual impact and messaging.

- Finding more friends and followers leads to a larger network of opportunity.

- Participate in Twitter chats to build reach.

- Stay on topic with content—content you want to be associated with, that is.

- Optimize your Twitter schedules with tools like Buffer.

"If you want to improve your social influence, a good place to start is by focusing your efforts on becoming more engaging. If you can engage users, then you have the ability to influence them. So how do you get people to engage with you? Interact with them and be interesting! Remember, it takes two to tango. The more you engage with other people's content, the more likely they'll engage with yours."

–Michelle Marie (plus.google.com/u/0/+MichelleMarie/posts), social media strategist selected by Google as one of the "Most Fun & Interesting" people to follow on Google+ with a placement on Google's elite Suggested User List (SUL) with more than 1.5 million followers on Google+.

Who Wins, and What's the Score?

Klout's (klout.com/corp/score) average score is "about 40." Among registered Klout users, a score of 63 puts you in the 95th percentile. A Kred score of 600+ puts a user in the top 21%. A score of 800+ would be top 0.1%. The average score is not published for "Global Kred," but Kred does show the average scores for each "Community" on the Community pages.

So, what's Klout got to do with it? Everything. And nothing.

Social PR Secret
New to the influence scoring scene is ClearVoice (http://www. clearvoice.com/), a platform that helps content producers (that's you!) measure influence using a scoring system, profile and a means to build authority and gain more influence in your field.

Why Is Influencer Marketing Effective?

Danielle Wiley knows better than most why influencer marketing has become so increasingly popular over the years. When she realized that companies were spending too many hours and fees looking for influencers and influencers didn't want to handle the business aspect of the arrangement, an idea was formed.

Her company, Sway Group, was created for the sole purpose of providing a "middle man" between companies and influencers. Danielle has first-hand knowledge seeing the positive benefits in influencer marketing between her own clients.

She notes that influencer marketing is effective because the relationship is two-fold—that is, it "gives brands reach within their target demographics and an influencer holds a lot more weight and trust for products." The belief is that influencers will not agree to endorse or promote a product they personally don't believe in.

Other alluring perks of influencer marketing include:

- Cost Effective: Marketers who implemented an influencer marketing campaign earned an average of $6.85 in media value for every $1 they spent on paid media.

- High ROI: 81% of marketers say influencer marketing is effective.

- Gaining Consumers Trust: 92% of consumers trust recommendations from personal connections, while only 33% trust ads.

- Has Mass Popularity: 74% of all marketers plan to use influencer marketing

Social PR Secret
Social media popularity (in terms of number of friends and followers) does not equate to influence. It's more about having the ability to move content through an engaged network and influence someone to take an action.

Chapter 18
Measurement, Analytics, and Google

Measuring Up to What Matters

How often are you looking at your analytics? Pre-Internet PR was pretty weak when it came down measurement. The biggest challenge was explaining and defending the value of public relations.

Back in the old PR days, when we first started working on a new account, one of the first things we'd do is start a clipping book. Every time a media story came out, it was placed in the clipping book and the thicker, the better. These were one of the main ways to measure how traditional PR tracked media coverage in print or broadcast. What did this equate to in sales and financial terms? The answer: the PR industry turned to advertising media equivalents, so a full-page article would be valued at the equivalent of a one-page ad. Thus, there wasn't a black-and-white way to measure the true value of public relations.

Hello Internet, Search Engines, and Social Networks

Measurement: a big breakthrough in PR and one of the industry's biggest challenges. Today, the data is available to learn what social PR content drives conversions with social audiences, as well as search engines and online media. At the very minimum, every PR professional should have a basic understanding of Google Analytics and access to your brand's Google Analytics account. This is a necessity in today's world, plain and simple. You can find plenty of online tutorials on YouTube and even via Google should you need them.

Using data from platforms such as Google Analytics, we can measure the real social PR payoff, validate our services, make better decisions, and gather insights. The amount of measurement and analytics tools can be endless and you can easily spend all day looking at reports and pools of meaningless data, so you need a good plan. Here are a few:

- *Start with the basics first*: It all starts with the basic understanding of your owned properties, so begin with the web analytics of your owned media; your website and blog first, and then move to looking at other outside data analytics.

- *Measuring in all the right places*: At the end of the day, the most important analytics are what matters most to your business goals. This could be email sign-ups, subscriptions, product sales, media mentions, visits, or shares.

- *Today's social PR KPIs*: Setting key performance indicators (KPIs) prior to a Social PR campaign allows you to set benchmarks to measure against and helps get the "buy in" from all the decision makers. Make sure everyone (from the president to CMO to sales manager to marketing) is on the same page as to what the meaning of success looks like. Of course, the ultimate KPI is the actual sale or conversion (financial ROI) or the front-page story in *The Wall Street Journal* (many times ego-ROI), but there's a journey involved in that ultimate KPI win, a process of touchpoints, relationship building, and nurturing.

Social Public Relations Key Performance Indicators Examples:

- *Volume and Depth KPIs*: This could be the quantity of articles or the number of articles that communicate the brand's message.

- *Sentiment KPIs*: Tracking the percentage of positive or negative comments across the social and search graphs.

- *Engagement KPIs*: The number of @mentions, retweets, +1s, likes, shares, comments on articles, organic media reactions, etc.

- *Conversion KPIs*: This could be the number of email sign-ups as a result of a news release or number of white papers requested from a webinar.

Whatever the KPIs are, list them and be specific. Football is a great analogy for goals and objectives, so think of your objectives as the yards and downs along the way and the goals as your touchdowns. Make sure to set KPIs so you can keep score!

If you're using social media as a means to get publicity, visibility, and quality exposure, then tuning into Google Analytics' social media reports is vital to success, though this isn't a native skill to many communications professionals.

I can't think of a more perfect person to be a Product Marketing Manager at Google Analytics than Adam Singer (www.google. com/about/careers/lifeatgoogle/measure-by-measure-prod-uct-marketing-manager-adam-singer.html). He's extremely passionate about digital marketing and PR, technology and media companies, and anything new that connects us and allows better communication in our world. We not only share the same social

PR enthusiasm, but have also shared a few social PR conference panels together, spreading the good word about optimizing the PR and marketing process for better conversion. Today, Adam provides guidance through a host of industry webinars, blogs articulating insights on how the PR industry can best use Google's Social Analytics, as well as the publicity factors of a brand using Google+.

Social PR Secret Tips on Measurement

Two main points to measure using Google Analytics are: (1) referring traffic and (2) the full value of traffic coming from social sites and measure how they lead to direct conversions or assist in future conversions.

Social media and PR are typically in the early "dating" part of an organization's relationship building. On average, customers interact with a brand 4.3 times over a 2-day period before they finally make a purchase. Just like in the old days of PR, social media and PR may not get the full credit they deserve for those only looking at last-click attribution.

Social PR Secret

Think beyond the obvious KPIs such as number of followers and quantity of visitors. Instead, think about KPIs such as email sign-ups or newsletter subscribers, types of KPIs that could eventually lead to the ultimate KPI: a new client or customer.

Singer reminds marketers to pay attention to which networks are working best for your brand and adjust accordingly.

Watch the Social Flow via Google Analytics. This report starts with the source of traffic, such as Twitter and breaks down how many people stayed on the site to visit another page and which pages they visited. This illustrates how your website visitors that originated from a social network move through your site.

Social PR Secret
Keep in mind that Google has the largest audience and make sure your brand, organization, or client is set up properly and active on Google+ and YouTube.

Google+ influences how you look in search results in a visual way and is important from a PR perspective. You always want to own the first page of search and be proactive in the event of negative reviews or a bad online story.

When properly optimized and managed, Google+ can serve as an influence to positive reputation management for a brand.

Social PR Secret
On Google Analytics, use this custom Google Social dashboard: troni.me/GASocialDash

Social Dashboard Beyond Google

Be active on all the social sites that matter. Research what channels your audience likes best. Creating dashboards for the numbers and metrics that matter most will make your social PR life easier and result in better decision-making, budget planning, and accountability.

Social PR Secret
Check out social analytics dashboards that allow you to monitor beyond Google and across all social media channels and see what social PR content is having the most impact, while also recognizing your brand evangelists.
@Sendible
@Sumall
@Hootsuite
@Cyfe
@Quintly
@SproutSocial
@SimplyMeasured

While many social PR professionals are already measuring—in fact, we're swimming in numbers and reports—the question is: Who is doing this effectively and efficiently? Measuring what matters to the brand's business objectives is all that truly matters at the end of the day.

Here are some social reports I recommend you view once inside your Google Analytics. Start with Google Analytics > Traffic Sources > Social >, then:

> **Overview**: When the CEO asks for "Just the highlights please," the overview gives a 20,000 foot view of the visits coming to your website or blog as a result of social media.

> **Social Network Referrals**: Find out if you are working for social media or if social media is working for you. Do you get more traffic from Facebook or LinkedIn? Or is YouTube's average visit on your website higher than all social referrals? As your Social PR content is shared and people come to your site, it's important to understand how visitors from different sources engage with your site and also where they originate from.

Some more reports to check out include:

> **Conversions:** It's the ROI or bust! First, make sure you define what your business considers a conversion. This could be an email sign up, a form being filled out, a product order or some sort of a sale or even a download. Put monetary value on these conversions. Do you understand the impact of social media on your business?

> **Top Conversion Paths:** Did you ever wonder how many interactions happen before a sale is made and where social media fits into the journey of a conversion? One of my favorite Social PR reports is this visual snapshot of how your traffic sources work together to create sales and conversions.

> **Trackbacks:** Because you need to know who is linking back to your website. Get notified when another website or blog links to your domain's news content. Why is this important? It allows you see what Social PR news content is popular plus is the credibility, influence and SEO authority. Note: this is also an area for online brand reputation. Monitor your brand, even in social analytics.

> **Landing Pages:** Make it a priority to know which pages of content are being shared, where they're being shared, and how.

> **Social Plugins:** Be sure to add Social Plugin buttons to your site such as Google "+1" and "Pin" it buttons - and follow the content that is shared so you can replicate success.

> **Top Conversion Funnel:** Do you understand the sequence of interactions that happen before a conversion and how social media fits in? You can add a "social" filter to this report and share it with your CEO to prove exactly how social media factors into sales.

Social PR Secret

Looking for a visual way to report Google Analytics? Have Visually Google Analytics Report (create.visual.ly/graphic/google-analytics) automatically delivered to your inbox each week.

Check out websta.me/formerly known as Webstagram(websta. me/and Simply Measured (simplymeasured.com) for even more analytics.

Are you ready to measure news content success and report on what really matters to the CEO and bottom-line business?

Chapter 19
Avoiding a PR Disaster

Does the saying, "There's no such thing as bad publicity" apply to social media blunders gone viral? Your brand ending up as a gag skit on SNL because of a social media mishap is probably not part of your PR strategy.

If you think social media and PR are two different departments with separate agendas, think again. The good, the bad, and the ugly stemming from social media sentiments that bubble up to a brand are a direct reflection on the company's image, credibility, influence, visibility, and—if you're a public company or a company trying to raise money—your investors. In more cases than not, employees behaving badly by accident or intentionally have the formula for PR disaster. Now social media is part of the PR department, and it's their problem.

Zen of a Social Media Policy for Good PR

- *Your employees are social! Win or #FAIL*: As the popularity of social media grows, brands small and large must face the fact that the people with the closest connection to your organization—employees—are active on social channels. While employees can be your perfect brand advocates and evangelists, they can also burn your reputation when they lose control on social media networks.

- *The employee social media manual #Trending #HR #PR*: To mitigate that risk, develop a company-wide policy that clearly defines both acceptable and unacceptable behavior on social media and dictates how employees can effectively communicate your brand culture, voice, and message. Include guidelines about confidential and proprietary information and how each should be treated and balanced against the transparency that consumers increasingly expect from social media.

- *Social media training program #Breaking #Success*: The company picnic and holiday party just got bigger, wider, and riskier with social media snapshots landing on Facebook and Instagram. Is that a shot of tequila that the CEO is doing? Hello, front page news and PR hangover. Planning and determining who will provide your employees with these resources will take the guesswork out of determining what's appropriate to post, tweet, or share. It also increases the consistency of communications about your brand. Consider delivering educational resources to your employees as part of a company-wide social media training program.

The Road to ROI: Building Strategy for Social Marketing Success, speaks to how to influence the conversation without trying to control it. One of the key areas focused on in the report was the internal planning of social media and how that ties into the external public relations and reputation management of a company.

Your social media policy should specifically address these 11 questions:

1. What are the goals of your social media policy?

2. How will you update your policy and reinforce it?

3. What information about your business can employees share?

4. Which social networks will you maintain a presence on?

5. How will you monitor conversations about your brand on social channels? Who, specifically, will monitor these conversations?

6. How will you maintain a consistent social tone and style across these networks?

7. Will you encourage employees to participate in social media as a representative of your brand?

8. How will you respond to consumers who communicate with your brand through social channels? Who will respond on your brand's behalf?

9. Who is authorized to proactively post on your brand's behalf? Does this authorization account for different regions and teams?

10. What constitutes a social media "crisis" for your business? What is your process for handling a post that could be categorized as a crisis?

11. How will you educate your employees on the social media policy?

PR+: Social Media Policy Resources

- Social Media Policy Tool (socialmedia.policytool.net): When you can't wait for the red tape and need it quick, check out this streamlined process that merely requires you to answer a brief questionnaire and provides you with a complete social media policy customized to your company.

- Social Media Policy Database (socialmediagovernance. com/policies.php): Ever wonder what the social media guidelines look like for big brands like Coca-Cola, Nordstrom, or Walmart? Consider it done! This is the most complete listing of social media policies, referenced by the world's largest brands and agencies.

A key takeaway from Wildfire's report is to not treat social media as a silo. One of the biggest hindrances happens when social media is treated as separate category without collaboration and interaction from marketing, PR, and customer service. How does your social media policy measure up?

A portion of this chapter originally appeared in Search Engine Watch.

Chapter 20
Strategy for Tragedy

We interrupt this regularly scheduled program for...

The concept of brands becoming and acting more like editorial publishers is evident as organizations opt to do what the media is doing, focusing on what's actually happening in real-time in the news.

Do we really need to have this conversation? Truthfully I'd rather not, yet the tragedies such as the Orlando Pulse nightclub shooting, the largest mass shooting in the United States as of this publishing date, the Newtown, Connecticut shooting and the Boston Marathon bombings bring a new normal to a day in the life of a social PR professional. As tragedy unfolds, it's now our job to edit our social PR calendars to include the new, embrace the news, or remove our news from the social feed to allow room for what's most important.

When the unthinkable and unpredictable happens, life must still go on. As much as we wish the world could stop for a moment so we could collect our thoughts, business marches on.

I didn't choose to be in crisis management. It chose me when one of my best friends was murdered. I was just starting my career in PR and suddenly found myself, alongside my friend's family, under the spotlight of a tragic national news story. I understand all too well what those families are going through with what can seem like a circus of media.

Everywhere we look in the wake of tragedy, people and organizations struggle to express their acknowledgement or sympathies without crossing the boundaries that could make their messages appear self-serving or selfish. People are, by nature, skeptical of brand messaging.

Behind businesses are real people and, as people, we are all affected. The Pulse night club shooting attacked the GLBT community, the Newtown shooting attacked innocent elementary school students and teachers, and Boston bombings raise questions on how a brand should interact with fans during a crisis and the unwritten rules of social media etiquette.

Live video is now capturing news unfolding in real time like never before and the new normal is becoming more and more challenging.

How Can Brands Support Audiences on Social Media?

If you're debating the power of social media for PR power, here's more proof that it matters: about 50% percent of consumers think a brand's Facebook (mashable.com/category/facebook) page is more useful than a brand's website, a study by Lab42 suggests.

If a brand really wants to have a personal relationship with its audience and be seen as more than just a way to get coupons and giveaways, they need to offer more than promotional content.

Brands need to offer resources—that is, meaningful content. The first step is being real and getting personal.

Your brand needs to be real during a community tragedy:

- *Be human*: Acknowledge what's happening, if that's appropriate and agreed internally.

- *Be real*: Stop automated posts. Get in real time when tragedy strikes.

- *Be credible*: Report and share news, but confirm sources and facts (on.fb.me/1oK2jQf) first.

- *Be caring*: Consider sensitive subject matter. If your brand is part of the tragedy or in a related industry, take a close look at what you're reporting.

- *Be considerate*: Take a few days off from your normal editorial calendar. Think about it—is anyone even paying attention to what you're promoting at that moment?

- "I typically recommend to cease posting branded content for the day, however always remain active in the community (regular moderation responsibilities)," writes social media and PR specialist Lisa Grimm (bit. ly/1AelxGi) in a heartfelt blog post she published the day of the Newtown shooting.

- *Be alert*: Have a meeting with the communications team and put someone in charge of watching real-time news so you're aware of issues—good or bad—that can impact your community.

- *Have a clean slate*: Consider taking down recent postings that might be offensive to current events.

Why Brands Shouldn't Ignore Tragedy

Sadly, I know what it's like to deal with the media surrounding a national story and be the target for interviews. The reason the collective conscience is so affected by tragic events is precisely because so many, if not all of us, have experienced tragedy in our own lives. We can't help but be empathetic. We want to stop the suffering of those affected because we know how damaging it really is. This "we" includes business owners and management too.

Even if your customers were not directly affected, they certainly empathize with those who were. They may feel helpless, desolate, or even experience survivor's guilt.

According to a recent study, 70% of people get most of their news from friends and family on Facebook and 36% get most of their news links from friends and family on Twitter, with more of the Twitter crowd using a smartphone. If you are putting your content in the social newsfeed during tragedy, think about if it is relevant or just taking up newsfeed space.

You Can't Schedule Life, or Social Media

While scheduling tools are helpful, social media PR news isn't something you can set and forget. These are communities of people who interact in real time, and if you're lucky enough to have a community grow up around you as a brand, you should be just as plugged in as they are in order to strengthen your relationships and sustain your reputation.

Education and Strategy are Paramount

Let's face it: Social media is not always in the hands of accredited PR professionals with years of crisis management experience on their resume. Does your community manager know the answers to these questions?

Do we comment during a natural disaster or national tragedy? If so, what does doing so look like? Chances are that if they don't, then neither does the organization. Consider having a plan in place to take action such as:

- Cease all scheduled or planned content for a period of time.

- Check ad schedule and pull content promotion or campaigns for a period of time.

Check Your Sources, Even When It's Not a Tragedy

Brands are learning to become news content publishers, and are getting bruised and beat up along the way. The ones who succeed will follow journalism and communications best practices, regardless of the topic, by doing routine editorial fact-checking and confirming sources.

Social PR Secret

In a time of tragedy or crisis, check out sources and be sure to fact-check. The last thing you want to do is perpetuate misinformation.

Chapter 21
Optimizing an Event
for Social PR

Optimizing, socializing, and publicizing an event is about enticing attendees, but it's also about attracting and engaging the people who *cannot* attend, including the media, bloggers, and high-profile influencers.

This concept caught my eye when I shared a search marketing panel in London with digital PR expert, Mel Carson, who at the time, was the brand evangelist for the Microsoft Advertising Community. Carson presented a case study of Microsoft Advertising social media marketing strategy that went beyond sponsoring and attending conferences. Through live tweeting, blogging, sharing video interviews and capturing images of the conference, the event was brought to life for the people who were not in attendance. Attendees became promoters by covering the event as on-the-spot journalists.

Help position yourself as a thought leader for industry news sources by using social media outlets to report on your company's branded events or other industry conferences. This can be an effective social PR content strategy. It boils down to building an online social media news hub around your offline activities; ultimately creating a platform for your online audience to enjoy and interact with the brand.

Your Social PR Event Action Plan

The Microsoft Advertising Community team had been using social media as a vehicle to listen to, educate, support, and market to customers and potential customers since 2006.

In the case study Carson shared, they created a robust "on-the-ground plan" that outlined hour-by-hour which sessions they'd be blogging about or tweeting from. It also included a detailed film schedule of interviews with conference delegates and speakers, as well as Microsoft's own executives.

This all helped to bring the event to life in real-time for the thousands of interested media, bloggers, advertisers, marketers and creatives who could not make the trip.

What was the result? They chalked up more than 40,000 interactions or "brand engagements" with branded coverage. That equates to people reading blog posts, watching videos, browsing photos, and engaging with them on Twitter.

Keeping the content relative, insightful, and actionable proved to be a winning combination for Microsoft and can work for your brand as well! Think about it: News nuggets delivered in innovative ways resonate with audiences on the social platforms and devices they are using at the time that's most convenient for them. Here are some forms of live, from-the-action content that a business can utilize:

- Live tweeting
- Live blogging

- Google Hangouts On Air turned into YouTube video interviews of speakers and industry experts

- Instagram images of the speakers with key messages as captions

- Sharing images on Facebook, Instagram, Pinterest and Tumblr

In using the above content types to promote your event before, during, and after, keep these things in mind:

- Basically, you are newsjacking the event.

- Leverage your social media platforms on brand publications to showcase event/industry influencers as part of your event content strategy.

- After the event, create strong visuals using slideshows to tell the story of the event and create infographics with fun facts about your event.

- Optimize all social content with appropriate hashtags, keywords, and links to reap the full benefits.

In Microsoft's case study, they didn't just consider Facebook or Twitter when promoting one of their newest products because they considered the entire Internet as part of the social and mobile media landscape.

"The way I see it, social media is the Internet," Carson explains, "The Internet is inherently driven by social and now navigated by mobile."

Using a "social veneer" across all platforms:

Carson explains that blogs, search, and basically anything you can find on the Internet that has a social component to it are all valuable tools in your next social PR campaign.

Rather than considering different platforms as individual elements, apply a "social veneer" to your entire online public relations campaign; whether it be on mobile, television, or the Internet. Instead of limiting your focus to how to use social media in your next PR campaign, think broader and use the entire Internet experience by incorporating multiple platforms in order to make your campaign stand out.

Bringing the event to life/optimizing social PR for the event:

"Your goal should be to bring the event alive for your global audience," Carson states. You do that by creating excitement by posting content before the events even start. "Once there, make it your goal to connect to your Internet audience with lots of blogs, tweets, and photographs."

In social PR, the ultimate goal is to get your audience to share your content with others, thereby growing your own brand. It's up to you on how to make that happen and to make sure you provide the mechanism for them to share your content.

Keying in on social interaction KPIs:

Brand interaction is a key metric social PR pros can use to determine each campaign's reach. Every Tweet, comment, and video viewing related to a particular event campaign is an early indicator of how many people have interacted with your brand. Furthermore, this gives you a target audience for your next campaign or product launch. In Carson's experience, once you hook these people in, they'll rarely unfollow you if you deliver a rich content experience.

Strategically curating images and videos to publicize events creates a social PR library and historical timeline. Today there is no shortage of mobile cameras, but it makes sense to invest in professional photography and videography for every event as well.

The Social PR Secret

When putting together a presentation or event, don't just think of the people in the room. Rather, every tweet, blog post, image, or video you post online is for the media, bloggers, and people who *couldn't* make it.

Keep in mind that this person who could not make it could be a top-tier columnist, influential blogger, or industry reporter looking for expert sources or a prospect who is looking to research. Either way, you are starting to build relationships.

Whether it is a conference, grand opening event, or product launch, when it comes to social event PR, start the process before the event, keep it going at the event, and carry it on after.

This chapter originally appeared in and is also a contributing chapter in *Content Marketing Strategies for Professionals* by Bruce Clay and Murray Newlands. (www.bruceclay.com/blog/optimizing-an-event-to-attract-media)

Chapter 22
Social PR Collaboration #FTW

Social PR Collaboration: Change your workflow

Optimizing your workflow, now that's an interesting concept!

Maybe you've had a social PR day or two like this: With deadlines looming, you scour your computer/Dropbox/Google Drive for the latest version of a client's pitch for an upcoming meeting. While searching your overflowing inbox, you find that one email from the CEO to share with the freelance writer, and you're managing social media accounts and gathering research for the social media calendar and blog posts you need to finish by end of week. Oh wait, the media just called and wants to interview your boss in one hour. Everything you were planning comes to a stop, you switch gears, and what was supposed to get done today gets pushed to tomorrow.

Did you know… each time you are pulled off task, it can take 23 minutes to return to the original task with full focus? Gone. *Poof!*

Breakfast and lunch blur into intravenous episodes at Starbucks. Forget the gym, yoga, or drinks with friends, you realize the only way to possibly keep your head above water is to spend every night working and every day putting out fires.

Sound familiar? Been there, done that.

If you are in the business of social media and public relations—part-time, full-time, or anytime—chances are you get things done. I promise, you need a platform to keep all the balls up in the air, so it's time to think about social collaboration that works inside and *outside* your organization.

Social PR Truth or Consequences: Work Needs a Makeover

For most people, "work" is broken and the processes and platforms that used to get work done might need a makeover (or plastic surgery). Studies show that 48% of our week is spent on email. Yes, email. We spend, on average, 20% of our time looking for internal information and 28% of time managing email itself.[8]

Some experts suggest banning email entirely[9] or declaring email bankruptcy[10], alerting everyone in your electronic world that you're going for broke in your inbox and will be starting fresh.

I have tried to do this two years in a row, but instead, I archived my entire inbox and started putting systems and platforms in place to reduce the annoying and time-consuming method of searching for emails.

---

[8] (www.mckinsey.com/insights/mgi/research/technology_and_innovation/the_social_economy).

[9] (www.nytimes.com/roomfordebate/2011/12/05/should-workplaces-ban-e-mail-37hp)

[10] (www.npr.org/templates/rundowns/rundown.php?prgId=13&prgDate=02-16-2011

Besides email, most people use an average of nine apps per day to manage their work and personal lives. Forget chronic stress, now it's called "app fatigue." Single-use apps can do one thing really well, but that means you have to bundle multiple apps just to perform a common task.

Modern Cluster Fu*k

We're dealing with a cluster fu*k of modern technology. While it has led to significant productivity increases by virtue of technology's ubiquity, the amount of devices and apps are essentially driving us to distraction and possibly destruction. A Wall Street Journal article exposed the excessive amount of workplace distraction[11], citing new statistics that reveal we're interrupted every three minutes.

It's not what you know, it's what you don't know that you don't know

As social PR pros, it's time we check out of email rehab and fix our work. Let's reduce the number of apps we use and stop using email as a catch-all filing cabinet. Try a healthier dose of social collaboration tools instead—it can add free hours to your day. Yes, that yoga class or happy hour is now in sight!

With all this "work" talk, you might be asking yourself: Do I even have time to change my workflow?

Yes! As busy, multitasking PR professionals, can we afford not to?

Reframe the work involved to change, and instead embrace it. And find peace in knowing that by optimizing your workflow,

---

[11]   (online.wsj.com/article/SB100014241278873243392045781732522230
22388.html),

you can optimize your social PR productivity and gain more happy :) hours!

PR professionals are experts at optimizing, publicizing, and socializing for others. We have to be; it's our job. But we're often a little helter-skelter about how we get the real work done. There's always so much to do, so many fires to put out, and only so much of "us" to go around.

We lead our clients to employ social communication and public relations best practices. We know our stuff, and we're bold in our strategies. So why don't we wax eloquently on the way that work should be done? We need to take a stand for making our work lives more efficient and start offering additional advice that will help our clients in ancillary ways. "Step away from the 'reply all' button, folks; we're here to show you a better way!"

What is social collaboration anyway?

You've probably heard of and are possibly working with the Basecamps, HighRises or Asanas of the project management world, and that is a step towards internal collaboration and productivity. But I'm a big believer in an open social collaboration platform because it lets you operate outside the walls of your team and encourages you to collaborate with your clients, customers, and social circle. Plus, the best collaboration tools have public sharing components that make sharing the awesome work you've done even simpler.

It's estimated that 75%
(www.mckinsey.com/insights/mgi/research/technology_and_
innovation/the_social_economy)
of enterprise-level organizations will adopt a social collaboration platform in 2013.

According to analysts at Altimeter Group, enterprise collaboration drives business value in four ways[12]:

- **Encourages** sharing
- **Captures** knowledge
- **Enables** action
- **Empowers** people

By implementing a social collaboration and productivity platform to your social PR workday, you can:

- **Save time** spent managing media resources
- **Increase efficiency** in your efforts to garner media attention
- **Decrease the number of emails**, browser windows, and other tools used to produce content

Social PR Secret
If you don't value your time, neither will others. Stop giving away your time and talents – start charging for it. @KimGarst

How to find the right social collaboration tool

To really make work "work" and to find the right social collaboration tool, you'll need one that consolidates all your common tools into one online and mobile platform.

"Work" most often encompasses:

- Files/Documents
- Tasks
- Discussions/Comments

---

[12] (www.altimetergroup.com/research/reports/making-the-business-case-for-enterprise-social-networks)

- Email
- Calendars
- Working with other people (a.k.a. "collaboration"—especially for us PR pros!)
- Social networks

Here are some social collaboration platforms and systems I have used:

Asana (www.asana.com): A web and mobile application designed to enable teamwork without email. It was founded by Facebook's co-founder Dustin Moskovitz and ex-engineer Justin Rosenstein, who both worked on improving the productivity of employees at Facebook.

Basecamp (basecamp.com): The tag is "everyone's favorite project management system," and I know so many people that love Basecamp and swear by it. I tried it, paid for it for years, and never could get it to work for me. Instead, I felt like I was always working for Basecamp. But you know the saying, "user error," I am sure it was me and not Basecamp. I still work in it sometimes with partner agencies, but I do not miss it.

Ways you can use a social collaboration tool

There are more applications that I can list, but here are a few ways that you can integrate social collaboration in your social PR daily life.

Preparing for a conference/presentation: Whether you are presenting on a panel at conference or board meeting, moderating speakers for an event, or even coordinating the next PTA annual luncheon, why use email to communicate, coordinate, collaborate and mash up ideas? Your email is already littered with very important messages and spam.

Collaborative content creation: Content marketing is so important to us and our clients. but the process can be more iterative than we'd like it to be. I recommend working with your co-creators in real time within your collaboration platform. When you're ready, invite the final decision makers so they can approve content from within that task, thus eliminating emails (and providing better documentation).

Document sharing: I love Dropbox, but I don't prefer to use another file-sharing system outside of my task system. Version control of documents can be a real pain for social PR pros, so I'm all about creating or uploading a document within my platform and adding the appropriate recipients to the task itself. If I want to share it by email, I can still do that, but at least my document collaborators will be editing the document in real time in the track. No more looking for the latest version!

Social PR editorial planning: Create a shared calendar with everyone who contributes to your editorial efforts. Assign, brainstorm, and whatever else you typically do and set up a calendar everyone can view.

Your Social PR Life 2.0

I invite you to upgrade your social PR efforts with the concept of social collaboration. Because you're a doer. With social collaboration, you can become a better communicator and collaborator, while becoming more effective and efficient. And you'll have more time for happy hours. It's time to start collaborating. Think outside the inbox.

Chapter 23
Facebook PR Secrets for More Newsfeed Coverage

Is Facebook *blue* the new black for Community Managers? Social dashboards indicate Facebook marketing fashion changes by the season.

In order to stay ahead of the competition, you might have to download a book or two, attend a webinar or *five*, and stay on a regular diet that includes a healthy dose of the online marketing conference circuit.

You may also turn to trusted experts, the ones who spend their days and nights tracking, testing, and experimenting to find out the best colors, times, lengths, accessories, apps, and more to find this season's Facebook community manager dos and don'ts.

Two of the latest online marketing business books uncovered some Facebook fashion forward thinking designed with community managers in mind.

The Complete Social Media Community Manager's Guide by Marty Weintraub and Lauren Donovan (www.aimclearblog.com) along with *The Science of Marketing* by Dan Zarrella (danzarrella.com) offer latest top shelf insights, data, and tips when it comes to how a brand can rank in authenticity and pull some publicity out of its Facebook Page.

Today's community manager can double as a magazine editor by day and DJ by night, spinning content to match the mood, audience, and atmosphere of the daily Facebook newsfeed.

Use the 50/30/20 Rule

Weintraub and Donovan's spin on Facebook content calls for 50/30/20 rule.

1. **50 percent news.** Include a custom blend of **third party, non-competitive content** from sites such as AllTop.com and Buzzfeed.com industry.

2. **30 percent personality.** Highlight a **sparkle of strategic personalization** and personality with real-time journalism that can only happen on your Facebook page.

3. **20 percent business.** After you've given away all the friendship bracelets, it's time for business, and you can put on the most tasteful type of branded, self-promotional content.

The Art & Science of Facebook Marketing

Social media can be described as a cool blend of art and science, yet the proof is in the data according to Zarrella who notes these key findings when it comes to Facebook community manager formulas:

1. **Be positive.** The most shareable kind of content on Facebook is positivity and the least shared is negativity.

2. **Avoid unnecessary types of words.** Write simply. Aim for the fifth-grade level, rather than college level. Think *USA Today* rather than *New York Times*.

3. **Let your hair down.** Relax your corporate content and think outside of the boring cubicle world.

4. **High five!** For post frequency, Zarrella found in his research that the sweet spot is four to five times a week but recommends that brands use this as a starting point and experiment from there.

Should Community Managers go for the Facebook Reaction or Share?

Shares are the best for word of mouth A share means people endorse your content to the point of putting their reputation on the line. Your ad or post is interesting enough where people are willing to share it," said Dennis Yu (blitzmetrics.com), co-founder and chief executive officer at BlitzMetrics.

Timing is Everything on Facebook

The data from Zarrella underlines a recent study by Salesforce Marketing Cloud (www.salesforcemarketingcloud.com/resources/ebooks/strategies-for-effective-wall-posts-a-timeline-analysis):

Join the after-hours Facebook party: Brand posts published between 8 p.m. and 7 a.m., which are defined as "non-busy hours," receive higher interaction than those that post between 8 a.m. and 7 p.m., which are defined as "busy hours."

Weekends are made for Facebook: The interaction rate for posts on weekends is higher compared to weekday posts, however fewer posts are published on Saturdays and Sundays.

Less is More :D

And to go along with the proof that positive posts are better received than negative, just say it with a simple :).

1. **I ♥ Facebook!** Facebook posts that use emoticons receive **52% more Facebook fan engagement** and have a 57% higher like rate, 33% higher comment rate, and 33% higher share rate. Thumbs up and ♥ that.

2. **Less might be more on Facebook.** Brands that post one or two times per day see 19% higher interaction rates than those who post three or more times per day. The key is to not bombard fans with too many posts, as Facebook news feed optimization often penalizes for this.

3. **Paying to play.** Public relations and advertising used to be like church and state. Not anymore. When done right, promoting a brand's news content in Facebook via social advertising strategies such as custom audience targeting and remarketing website visitors or email lists can be an effective one-two punch for building community. It's super important that public relations content take advantage of the latest Facebook marketing strategies including paid.

Delivering Happiness on Facebook

Social PR lessons to be learned for Facebook community managers and brands can come from some not so recent, but not so distant, Internet entrepreneurs like Zappos CEO, Tony Hsieh, author of the book *Delivering Happiness: A Path to Profits, Passion, and Purpose*, which debuted in 2010 at number one on the *New York Times* Best Seller List and stayed on the list for 27 consecutive weeks.

What Facebook PR Secrets can Community Managers learn from Hsieh? These core values underlined on the Delivering

Happiness website may also be a secret formula to social PR community manager success on Facebook:

1. **Be true** to your (nerdie) self. Live with passion and purpose.

2. **Think, say, and do in harmony** and have consideration of others.

3. Communicate with **honesty** and respect.

4. **Have fun and think full.** 50% air + 50% water = 100% full.

5. **Inspire** and be inspired. Read more, talk less.

6. **Be humble**, be grateful.

7. **Build community** and meaningful relationships. Take more than you give.

8. **Keep your heart + mind open** and aligned. Keep growing and learning.

9. Be like MacGyver and Bruce Lee. **Do more with less**, be creative and adventurous, and fluid like water.

10. **Create change** in the world more than you ever thought possible.

Be Real

"Whether it's Twitter, Facebook, Snapchat, or whatever the next thing is, the easiest way to deal with everything is to just encourage employees to be real and use their best judgment," Hsieh said.

Facebook community managers are tasked with balancing the art and science of Facebook PR and marketing. Do you have a Facebook PR secret to share?

Chapter 24
Instagram PR Secrets: Like, Watch, Stop, and Scroll

You don't have to be Kylie Jenner or Justin Bieber to be an Instagram master. I sat down with Krista Neher, author of *Visual Social Marketing for Dummies*, to learn more about the popular visual social networks, like the explosively famous Instagram, and how to use them best to market your business.

Owned by Facebook, Instagram was launched in October of 2010 by Kevin Systrom and Mike Krieger and is currently one of the most popular photo-sharing social media networks. Known for its square-shaped photos and large selection of photo filters, Instagram recently added a video sharing option and social ad opportunities for maximum experience.

It's Not About You, It's About Your Community

If you look at your Instagram account like it's a magazine your community is subscribing to, then planning the content becomes easier and starts to make more sense. The mistake many brands (small, large, and personal) make is that they focus their Instagram messaging about themselves too much and not enough about their community's needs, wants, or interests. It's not about your every waking brand's moment; it's about your audience's hopes, desires, needs, dreams, and fears.

What About My Business?

According to Krista, before getting lost in all of the cropping, filters, editing, and posting, you should ask yourself these questions to make sure that your company belongs on a visual social media site:

- **Is your audience there?** This is the most crucial question to ask when deciding if you want to use any of these sites. Instagram's demographics, for example, mainly consist of young adults of both sexes. If your audience is over 30, Krista says it may be best to focus on other sites before jumping into these.

- **Do I have the resources to post consistently?** Instagram, for example, timestamps your posts and has a very fast-paced feed. To gain popularity, then, you need to be able to post multiple times per week.

- **How to take my brand visual?** Sometimes, deciding when to get on visual marketing is a matter of immense creativity. Will your brand look good in photos? For example, Starbucks recently held a competition on Instagram, encouraging its customers to decorate their Starbucks cups in creative patterns and upload the images. If coffee can look good in photos, there's a way for your brand to do it, too!

Instagram PR Secrets by Krista Neher

How often should I post? I always say that you get out what you put in. Aim to post a few times a week. If you have a very visual business, you can post as much as a few times a day.

Pro Tip for Hashtags: Keep your description short and to the point and "hashtag bomb" the first comment. Hashtags are the only searchable content on Instagram.

Instavideo: Instagram recently increased video length to 60 seconds. Facebook is investing heavily in video content and it wouldn't be surprising for Instagram to follow suit. Facebook also prioritizes video in the algorithm.

Automation Tip: Don't use the buttons in Instagram to post to other social networks (Twitter or Facebook Profile). Instead, automate with something like IFTTT so your Instagram photos show up as native images on these networks.

Grow your following: Participate in the community; pay attention to other people and they will pay attention to you. Like, comment on, and follow other photos and accounts to draw attention to yourself. Do it in a natural way; don't be spammy.

Inside Instagram

Algorithms Rule Content – Similar to Facebook, Instagram announced an algorithm in the timeline to change the order of content to show you what you are most likely to be interested in. Apparently, average Instagrammers only see 70% of potential photos, so the new change will show them the content they are most interested in first. What does this mean to you as a Social PR pro? Good content matters on Instagram, and you'll need to drive engagements and interest to maintain your reach. Hang on to the organic opportunity while it's still there.

Finally! Account Switching – If you've been on Instagram for business since the early days, you might have felt the frustration of having to log in and out of multiple accounts. Recently, Instagram announced account switching for mobile, and you can now switch between multiple accounts, making it easier to manage multiple accounts.

#InstaMeets

As the Instagram community has grown around the world, so too has the occurrence of InstaMeets: gatherings of people coming together to connect, explore, and celebrate their creativity.

Instagram Ads

If you can't wait to grow organically and have a budget to put behind Instagram Ads, hop over to Facebook Ads Manager for Insta exposure.

Instagram Contests

The best place to get publicity is directly from your audience, and the power of user-generated content (UGC) has never been more valuable. With over 70 million media posted every day, Instagram is, without a doubt, the kingdom of user-generated content. Think about how your brand can benefit from that to generate attention, connect with customers and more influencers, engage community, and generate authentic content. Shortstack (@ShortstackLab) recommends these four things before running a contest in order to get maximum publicity for your brand:

1. **Think about the type of photo contest you want to run** - Like-to-Win, Comment-to-Win, Photo Challenge, or Repost-to-Win are some examples.

2. **Write your contest rules** - Be sure to post them on your website

3. **Give away a relevant prize** - There is nothing worse than giving away a prize that is not synergistic with your brand. Making this mistake can be bad PR and will create a false positive of increasing follower rate but the followers are not a good match to your brand.

4. **Spread the word** - Use hashtags to increase exposure and cross-promote the contest on other social media channels.

Insta Tips, Tricks, and Tools

Make your bio count - What are you offering? Share your purpose, intention, and passion. Most importantly, think about the URL you want in your bio and change it according to what you are currently promoting or featuring.

Be a creative director - Instagram is your online magazine, and you're in charge. Be sure to have a plan that curates and creates the best visual experience your followers will not just like but love.

Filter it! But pick the right one - Filters that get more likes and overall engagement are as follows:

- Mayfair
- Inkwell
- Amaro
- Walden
- Lo-Fi

Hashtags #FTW (For The Win) - Without a hashtag, you will significantly decrease your chances for visibility. Unlike Twitter, the more hashtags the better with Instagram. Interactions are highest on Instagram posts that include 11+ hashtags, according to a study done by Buffer. (Don't stress too much on the quantity of hashtags, just be sure to use quality hashtags that make sense.)

Social PR Secret

Subscribe to Instagram's business blog so you are first to know about new features or changes.

Instagram Social PR Tool Box

- Iconosquare

- Shortstack

- Gramfeed

- Canva

- Instabrand

- Snapfluence

Social PR Secret

There's a ton of incredible content to curate and share from Instagram. My favorite way to do this and give credit is to use the app called Repost. One of my fave accounts is @MuradOsman, who started the famous #followmeto hashtag.

Sources

selfstartr.com/instagram-marketing-tips-ecommerce

www.shortstack.com/4-things-you-must-do-before-hosting-an-instagram-contest

blog.bufferapp.com/a-scientific-guide-to-hashtags-which-ones-work-when-and-how-many

Chapter 25
Snapchat Secrets, Stories, and Savviness

"We are not the sum of everything we have said or done or experienced or published—we are the result. We are who we are today, right now."
— *Evan Spiegel, CEO of Snapchat, at the AXS Partner Summit in January 2014*

When Snapchat launched in 2011 by Stanford University students Evan Spiegel and Bobby Murphy, the first users to embrace the mobile messaging app were mostly high school students. Originally named Picaboo, then renamed Snapchat for the official Apple iOS launch, it was designed for mobile chat with the alluring feature of sending and receiving photos that then disappeared in real-time.

Spiegel wrote the following mission statement in the company's first blog post. "Snapchat isn't about capturing the traditional Kodak moment. It's about communicating with the full range of human emotion—not just what appears to be pretty or perfect."

Quite the opposite of social media platforms like Facebook or Instagram, what happens on Snapchat never stays on Snapchat—or anywhere. Well, sort of. If you're a hoarder and love to collect all your published images, good and bad, "just in case," Snapchat might be challenging for you to embrace.

Dubbed the "sexting app" for a period of time, Snapchat has put that stigma to bed with a positive reversal of fortune and reputation. The mobile app is now widely accepted by all ages. A comScore report declared that Snapchat is "breaking into the mainstream," estimating that 38% of U.S. smartphone users ages 25 to 34 are on Snapchat, and 14% of those 35 or older. Three years ago, those numbers were 5% and 2%, respectively. An estimated 14% of U.S. smartphone users 35 or older are on messaging app.

It's no longer a big deal that all photos and videos disappear after a predetermined amount of time ranging from 3 to 10 seconds, which is set by the sender. It's actually the new normal. Users have a variety of ways to hack the system and snatch photos after their intended time by taking a screenshot or now downloading into a more legit hub called Snapchat Memories.

In 2012, Snapchat sent 25 images per second, according to company officials. What were they sending? Snapchat's teen user base reported using it as a new way to pass notes in class such as behind-the-back photos of teachers and funny faces.

At the beginning of 2013, Snapchat's users sent 60 million messages daily, which increased to 400 million messages daily in November of that year. This was enough to grab the attention of Facebook founder and CEO Mark Zuckerberg, who offered to pay $3 billion in cash for Snapchat. This was followed by another offer by Google for $4 billion. Spiegel declined both lucrative offers and moved on to put his bets on raising money for Snapchat's growth and holding on to Snapchat's destiny. The media and investment communities were shocked at the offers, as well as the fact that the twenty-something Snapchat founders declined them.

Pioneer brands to open up shop on Snapchat included Taco Bell, the UFC, the New Orleans Saints, Mashable, and Rebecca Minkoff. They all saw Snapchat as an opportunity to have a two-way conversation with younger and harder-to-reach customers. Its little to no cost of interacting via snaps was a huge plus to marketers when compared to the high cost of traditional advertising.

In 2015, it was reported that 6 in 10 people, ages 13 to 35, in the United States were using Snapchat. Was that sustainable? Snapchat started heating up inside and out. The company began marketing to a new demographic—35 and older—showcasing its yellow, ghost-like logo on billboards in places like Los Angeles, Seattle, Tampa, and cities across the United States. When Snapchat was asked, "Why the billboards?" they responded, "Fun and awareness."

All of a sudden, a surge of 30, 40, and 50-year-olds were turning to their sons, daughters, nieces, nephews, and interns to show them how to work Snapchat. For one thing, Snapchat is lacking—purposeful or not—in instructions or a help tab. It's almost like, if you weren't on Snapchat from the beginning, good luck figuring it out.

As of 2016, Snapchat caught up with Facebook in video views, and all signs show it's destined to surge forward. Once shunned by brands as a shiny new object that was mostly kids' play with no marketing value, the tides have turned for Snapchat, making it the app to watch in 2016 and beyond.

The Snapchat rebirth caught on at 2016 SXSW as marketers rallied around the mobile marketing opportunity. Iconic social media marketer and brand evangelist for Apple, Canva, and Mercedes-Benz, Guy Kawasaki, linked up with Snapchat storyteller, influencer, and celebrity Mike Platco for a how-to tutorial via Facebook Live.

To say digital marketers are obsessed by Snapchat might be an understatement or an overstatement depending on whom you talk to. Best-selling author and entrepreneur Gary Vaynerchuk snapped into the Snapchat storytelling: "Going all in!" The brash and bold @GaryVee says he's been talking about Snapchat since 2013; he's just getting louder as of 2016. Vaynerchuk said in an interview in 2013, "Snapchat is one of the most successful marketing tools with my brand personally." Okay, then!

What's Different About Snapchat?

For starters, the first screen of the app is a camera, prompting us to share what we're seeing or doing in real time. We can decide whether to send our snap directly to friends (like a direct message), where it disappears after it's been watched (unlike a direct message), or post it to our Snapchat Story (sort of but not really like a Facebook post), where it can be viewed for 24 hours by a broader audience and then disappears (unlike any other social media platform).

Snapchat Haters?

Not all marketers are going "all in," however. Mark Fidelman is one of them. He published a Snapchat article on *Forbes*, along with a video interview, passionately stating why Snapchat was a loser when it comes to marketing. His reasons for hating on Snapchat can really be applied to any social network with similar drawbacks because Snapchat lacks what every marketer looks for in a social media marketing platform:

1. **No Staying Power.** Marketing that disappears? Not many brands or marketers can get past the fact that there is no repeat, repurpose, or actual save button.

2. **Growth Challenges.** It's extremely difficult and time-consuming to build a following on Snapchat without a push from a Snapchat celebrity. Snapchat seems to be taking note of this by its recent adding of giving users individual URLs to promote their account. However, compared to YouTube or Facebook, this is quite antiquated.

3. **No Links**. No outgoing links plus no possibility for referring traffic. This is a biggie for marketers. Unless you're one of the big brands on Discover, long-form content is not possible, and there's no way to add hyperlinks to drive traffic back to your owned media such as your website or blog.

When Mark published his article, I shared it on Twitter. Little did I know that this would trigger a heated discussion between @MarkFidelman and one of my followers. twitter.com/lisabuyer/status/705224694165860352

Snapchatology

- **Snaps:** A snap is a photo or video (up to 10 seconds long) taken via the Snapchat app. You can draw on a snap, create captions, add emojis, use filters, or add a feature called lenses. Snaps can be sent direct to another Snapchat user (lasts up to 10 seconds once opened) or added to your Snapchat story (lasts 24 hours).

- **Stories:** Stories are the daily collection of your public snaps that play back in chronological order. Snapchat launched "My Story" in Fall 2013. This turned out to be an overnight success for the Snapchat universe. By adding a Snap to your Story, it lives for 24 hours before it disappears, making room for the new.

- **Discover:** In early 2015, Snapchat introduced "Discover," a way for editorial teams from brands such as *Cosmopolitan*, Buzzfeed, and even *The Wall Street Journal* to produce premium content and make money from Snapchat readers through advertisements. Snapchat Discover publishers have built teams of editors, video producers and artists to create premium videos each day. Consistent with Snapchat mode: every channel of Discover is refreshed after 24 hours—what's news today is history tomorrow, of course!

- **Video Chat**: Snapchat offers a two-way private video chat. Just find one of your friends in your Snapchat inbox, swipe right, and start chatting. (For a video chat, you and the friend you want to chat with must both be using the app at the same time.) Snapchat's chat feature is a savvy customer service messaging tool for brands. Watch this video to learn more: youtu.be/UvhiRIT5DvU

- **Community Geofilters:** Calling all designers and artists. Snapchat wants your Geofilter designs (no brand logos allowed).

- **Branded Geofilters:** Having an event or business? Make the Geofilter yours! Now you can create your very own Snapchat Geofilter whether it's a wedding, party, conference, organization, or business (logos allowed). You can even step up your personal branding by creating your very own geofilter when attending a conference or event. For all the details on making your own geofilter, visit the Snapchat link. **www.snapchat.com/on-demand**! What a way to crowdsource the branding and publicity of an event or business!

- **Live Stories:** A collection of localized user-generated Snaps curated by the Snapchat team. This is where Snapchatters unite to share different perspectives on the same event or milestone. Los Angeles and New York were the first cities to receive live stories, and now Snapchat is working with broadcast rights holders like the UFC, the NFL and even the Olympics to bring if there's a major event happening, you can in your location and be the first "on the scene" thanks to the Snapchat community.

- **Lenses:** Selfie perfection is not the place for Snapchat; it's all about the raw, real, and ridiculous. If you're looking to Photoshop and then post the selfie you wish you were, move on to Instagram or Facebook. Snapchat's lenses are coined as the whole new way to see yourself(ie). When you're using the camera to take a selfie, just press and hold on your face to activate Lenses. You can play with Lenses before taking a Snap: just select one from the row at the bottom and follow the on-screen instructions.

- **Memories:** Photo hoarders rejoice. Snapchat introduced Memories as a way to save Snaps and Stories for future use or private viewing only.

Social PR Secret
Make sure to update your app regularly for new lenses!

- **Snapcodes:** As of today, discovering and searching for people or brands on Snapchat isn't easy. Snapcodes—

AKA Snaptag QR codes—offer one possible way to get the Snapchat word out by cross-marketing your own personal Snapchat QR code via your other social channels. Like we said, Snapchat doesn't make it easy for newbies. Using the Snapcodes or Snapchat URLs are the main ways to add or be added.

Social PR Secret
Download (http://thenextweb.com/apps/2015/05/04/you-can-now-download-your-snapchat-qr-code-to-customize-it/) your own Snapcode and customize it!

- **Campus Stories:** They are special, they are live, and they are created exclusively for college campuses. In other words, you won't see a campus story in your Snapchat story feed unless you are actually "on campus." According to the official Snapchat website: "Only Snapchatters whose phones indicate they're in and around a campus or were there in the last 24 hours, are able to post to and view the Campus Story. Campus Stories are a special place to share and see what is happening on your campus."

Want more? Check out the Snapchat support page.

Finding Friends and Followers on Snapchat

There are multiple ways to find and add friends on Snapchat, but the Discovery aspect is lacking when compared to Facebook or Instagram, for example. There isn't a way to search for people or brands on Snapchat. You must know the Snapchat users' exact name to find them, have their phone number in your contact list, and add them via the Snapchat URL link or using the Snapchat QR code.

How to Build Your Snapchat Audience

If you're a brand with deep pockets, like Disney World, you can hire a Snapchat celebrity to "take over" your account and quickly get the word out to build your audience. Otherwise, the best way is to promote your Snapchat account across your other social platforms and offline forms such as newsletters, signs, events, ads, billboards, and packaging.

Measuring Snapchat

True to form of Snapchat's other characteristics, measuring Snapchat is also a slight disappearing act. You can measure your individual Snaps and Stories, but as soon as they disappear, so do the analytics. Third-party platforms are beginning to pop up, including the Delmondo agency's Snapchat Analytics tool that is available to select brand and media partners. Brands making Snapchat-only offers—for example, creating a promo code only promoted on Snapchat—can measure the ROI and see how many actually redeem the offers. Advertisers on Snapchat are privy to more dynamic statistics, but marketers still have some options to gauge Snapchat success. Forget looking in Google Analytics or social media management platforms like Hootsuite or Sprout Social.

Nick Cicero, CEO of The Delmondo Agency, advises looking at these starting list metrics when measuring your Snapchat story. His His advice comes to us from his ebook that first introduce measurement strategies to brands on Snapchat, *The State of Snapchat Analytics*.

1. **Total Unique Views**: The number of people who have opened up the first frame in your Snapchat story for at least a second.

2. **Story Completions**: The number of people who have viewed the last Snap to measure the number of people who have completed your entire story. The more people who viewed the last frame of your story, the more people who have watched it all the way through and consumed that content.

3. **Completion Rate**: How many people actually watched all your complete stories versus each chapter (Snap).

4. **Screenshots**: This can be a way to measure engagement.

5. **Total Snaps Posted**: How many Snaps did the account create over the past time period? (e.g., 24 hours, week-over-week, month-over-month, etc.)

6. **Day Posted**: What day of the week was the Snap posted?

7. **Type of Content**: Is it a photo or a video?

8. **Art**: Is there a drawing or no drawing? Was there an emoji or no emoji?

9. **Text**: Is there text or no text?

10. **Length of Content**: How long is each frame of the Snap?

11. **Total Length**: The length of a complete Snapchat Story, found by exporting the story, saving it, and turning it into one video file.

12. **Total View Count**: The number of unique views on a Snapchat story.

13. **Starting View Count**: The number of views in the first frame of a Snapchat story

14. **Ending View Count**: The number of views in the last frame of a Snapchat story (also knowns as total Story completions).

15. **Screenshots**: The number of times someone has taken a screenshot of your photo.

16. **Link Clicks**: Aside from the chat feature, there's not—as of now—a real way for users to click outside of Snap-chat. One way to test can be integrating links into the content and trying to drive people to a mobile site, but we'll emphasize that it's a really clunky and terrible user experience.

Snapchat Trickery, Magic, and Wizardry

Go Direct, Gain, and Grow: Use Snapchat's personalized URLs and Snapcodes to gain followers and grow your community.

Master the Camera Flip Mid-Snap: Did you know you can switch between front-facing and rear cameras with a quick double tap on the screen? Tap, tap. Yes. Snap to it with creativity and perspective.

Filters for Snapchat PR: Take advantage of this personal or business branding and PR opportunity and get creative with Snapchat's Geofilters. Submitting is a snap, but be sure to follow the guidelines.

Snapchat Art: "This platform is forcing us to be very creative in a different way," Gary Vaynerchuk said in his SXSW 2016 keynote. It's true: Snapchat created a whole new language of creativity, so it's no surprise that the growing trend is Snapchat artistry. Why? It combines the perfect blend of visual, mobile, and social. If you have a knack for design and creative fun or even if you don't, get busy and stand out in the Snapchat universe using the draw tool, filters, and emojis.

Snapchat Influence: If you can't beat 'em, hire 'em. You don't have to be a big brand like Disney or Jolly Rancher to find a Snapchat influencer to help build your Snapchat community and get noticed.

Let the Music Play: Improve the mood of your Snaps and Stories by playing a song from Spotify while producing Snapchat videos.

Frequency Rules and Being Real: There's no frequency rule on Snapchat. Once, twice, or seven days a week can all work. But, the more storytelling you do, the more of a chance that you will end up at the top of your Snapchat community's latest Story. If you are going to be frequent, be real, authentic, and relevant.

Host a Q+A on Snapchat: What burning question and answers can you share with your audience? Ask your audience, but only give it away on Snapchat. If you share all the same info on all of your social networks, nothing is special, and everything is a rerun. Make your Snapchat storytelling authentic and unique to Snapchat.

Ask for It! Building community and getting the ROI have one thing in common: Asking for what you want. If you want people to spread the word about you on Snapchat or take advantage of your promo code, you must have a call to action.

Celebrity Status: You don't have to be Kylie Jenner (username: kylizzlemynizzl) to become a Snapchat celebrity. Look at how the early YouTube stars made their claim to fame. Most did it without the fancy optimization marketing tricks; they did it by putting their authentic persona forward.

Theme It: It could be as easy as talking about specific brands, DIY tips, behind-the-scenes, or even a tip of the day on something you're passionate about.

Artful Filters, Lenses, Emojis, and Doodle: Snapchat doodling is becoming an art form and filters are another aesthetic way to add uniqueness to a Snap and lenses add a playful way to mood-ify your brand's voice.

Blog It: Write about your Snapchat stories in your blog. Download some of your favorite stories and upload them to your YouTube channel called Favorite Snapchat Stories. Embed the Snapchat Story in the blog post

Mention in Bio, Profile Pic, About Us, Email Signature, Etc.: Put yourself out there if you want to build your audience on Snapchat. Be sure to let the world know how to find you on Snapchat via your most scalable places.

Social Teasers: Weave in teasers about Snapchat features and stories that you want to promote so that your audience knows they can only find it on Snapchat. I love the idea of a University of Florida professor giving study guide tips for the final exam only on Snapchat. Inspirational Brilliance.

Snapcash: On the money. Snapchat has one eye one commerce. Snapchatters can easily exchange money.

5 Reasons Marketers Obsess Over it

1. **POV and Storytelling:** Once you figure out the mechanics of Snapchat, you will find that you can create a series of daily stories. A not-so-well-known brand but very on point is BraVe Media Ventures (+braveventures on Snapchat). They share themed stories on Snapchat across a different point of view on different topics of employees and associates.

2. **Influencer Takeovers:** For brands just starting out and trying to gain reach quickly, a smart Snapchat strategy is tapping into a Snapchat celebrity to do a "takeover." Cicero explains the steps on how to use Snapchat to grow your audience on the Delmondo blog. Add NickCicero on Snapchat and subscribe to his company Delmondo's newsletter for weekly updates on the latest and greatest that Snapchat has to offer.

3. **Audience:** If your audience is on Snapchat, then reach them by being on the same social channel. Isn't this Step 1 in the social media strategy plan? Is the advertising and targeting there like Facebook? No. Is this a time to experiment and dive in if your audience is on Snapchat? Yes. If you're still not sure about this whole "social media" thing and are still trying to figure out what Instagram is, then maybe this is not the article or decade for you to be in marketing and public relations.

4. **Online Marketing:** While search marketers might still be trying to figure out the Google's next algorithm change, the thought of Snapchat as a way to influence search marketing is something that should be added to the radar. Delmondo is bullish on how Snapchat can influence search and drive quality traffic to a website, blog, or online publication.

5. **Public Relations:** Snapchat is real-time. Sexting could be a public relations nightmare, but let's just say that we are beyond this as a reason a brand should not experiment with Snapchat. There are more pros than cons starting with a way to instantly get news out to followers to connecting with the media in an instant way using Snapchat's chat feature, to communicating with clients and teams.

Snapchat Inspiration

Mashable: The always trending and inspirational.

Gary Vaynerchuk (@GaryVee): Giving new meaning to going all out with entrepreneurship and social media and bullish on Snapchat.

BraveVentures (www.snapchat.com/add/braveventures): For POV inspiration and more.

Nick Cicero (www.snapchat.com/add/nickcicero): Add him to your Snapchat #SocialPRSecrets back pocket.

Delmondo – the first Snapchat Agency for brands (http://delmondo.co): Subscribe to their newsletter and blog.

Mike Platco (www.snapchat.com/add/mplatco): Influencer and Snapchat storyteller with a knack for artistry. He's known for building the branded Snapchat account for Pretty Little Liars and helped launch the official Walt Disney World Snapchat account.

Shaun McBride (Shonduras): One of the Snapchat pros. His snaps run the gamut from hilarious illustrations to carefully plotted scenarios to building an interactive adventure with his Snapchat fans.

Mark Kaye (MarkKaye): Short-form video talent and inspiration, he's known as the Jimmy Fallon of Snapchat for the platform's first talk show, "Talkin Snap."

Disney: Goes big with a stream of pixie dust using influencers to take over the Snapchat account.

Taco Bell: Winning over Millennials with its of love using a Valentine's Day screenshot campaign.

W Hotel: Creative and well-branded geofilters put this brand on the Snapchat map.

UFC: Partners with Snapchat for Live Stories at their PPV events http://www.thedrum.com/news/2016/06/27/snapchat-partners-ufc-provide-live-stories-perspective-landmark-ufc-200-event

Starbucks. They received a latte love using a custom lens to kick off its loyalty card

Is Snapchat for your brand?

The first few years of Snapchat's history proved to be more for the immature and not so serious. Today, Snapchat is more than selfies and sexting. Disappearing anytime soon? Snapchat has gained ground and is zooming past Instagram for the teen market and is turning brands upside down as businesses try to figure out how to reach the Millennial market. Snapchat's 2016 growth spurt made it the buzz of Social Media Marketing World and the investment community with more than 100 million daily users who spend an average of 25 to 30 minutes on the app each day, Chief Executive Officer Evan Spiegel said in a 2016 presentation to bankers. About 60% of the daily users send content to friends or their stories.

It doesn't look like Snapchat is disappearing anytime soon.

Sources

en.wikipedia.org/wiki/Snapchat

snapchat-blog.com

fortune.com/2016/03/01/snapchat-facebook-video-views-2

www.snapchat.com/on-demand

www.convinceandconvert.com/social-media-measurement/ snapchat-measuring

www.brit.co/snapchat-tricks-tips-hacks

support.snapchat.com/a/geofilter-guidelinesLiquid   Self   concept snapchat-blog.com/post/61770468323/the-liquid-self

www.bloomberg.com/news/articles/2016-04-28/snapchat-us-er-content-fuels-jump-to-10-billion-daily-video-views?utm_ source=Delmondo+General&utm_campaign=d93e56f9e0-Del-mondo_Newsletter&utm_medium=email&utm_term=0_ df0aa02bca-d93e56f9e0-309618461

socialprchat.com/5-snapchat-pr-secrets-digital-marketers-are-flocking-to-snapchat-are-you

http://www.bloomberg.com/news/articles/2016-02-29/snap-chat-s-spiegel-to-investors-we-have-8-billion-video-views-a-day

Chapter 26
Pinterest PR Secrets

It's a fact. Social media and public relations posts that include images generate higher engagement, so it's not surprising that image-centric platforms such as Pinterest are garnering the attention of businesses large and small.

Pinterest, the third-largest social network in the U.S., was created by Ben Silbermann, Evan Sharp, and Paul Sciarra in March of 2010. An online visual "pinboard" that allows users to create boards on any topic and "pin" relevant images to them, this site has grown quickly in the last six years.

Pinterest, in particular, is perfectly set up for businesses to drive traffic and increase conversion. Here's why:

- Pinners are 47% more likely to experience a major life event within 6 months. They're also disproportionately using Pinterest to plan for these moments. As a result, they're more receptive to new ideas and new brands, and more likely to make major purchasing decisions based on images they collect.

- With 67% of the pins representing brands and products, Pinterest provides a great environment for retailers to cultivate relationship with consumers.

- Among pinners who have actively used Pinterest in the 6 months prior to this study, 96% reported that they used Pinterest to research and gather information. 93% reported that they used Pinterest to plan for purchases, and another 87% reported that their Pinterest engagement had helped them make their purchasing decision.

- Each "pin" that a user attaches to one of his or her Pinterest boards is worth, on average, 78 cents in additional sales to the brand whose merchandise is featured.

- Up to 47% of online consumers from the US have made online purchases based on Pinterest recommendations.

- The contextual relevance, made possible by the ability of a user to choose boards on a particular topic to follow, allows each pin to garner 4 times more revenue per click compared to Facebook or Twitter.

- From a purchasing psychology perspective, consumers use Pinterest as a means to construct their ideal selves. This encourages meaningful engagement between brands and consumers, which can help brands elevate from being considered as "commodity" to being "aspirational," thereby creating a unique positioning and building a loyal customer base in the process.

Despite the compelling stats, using Pinterest for business is still relatively new for most brands. In fact, only 17% of the Fortune 500 are active on Pinterest.

www.adweek.com/socialtimes/only-17-of-the-fortune-500-are-active-on-pinterest-study/634677

That means that smaller brands can take the opportunity to establish their presence and carve out space on this platform to cultivate a deeper relationship with consumers.

But you can't just stick some pretty pictures up and call it a day.

Like all social media platforms, there are strategies and tactics you can employ to make sure your effort pays off in the form of more quality traffic to your website that leads to increased conversion and revenue.

Let's look at 6 ways to drive traffic and increase conversion on Pinterest:

Create High-Quality, Evergreen Content

No matter what platform you're on, your Social PR content needs to be relevant, valuable, and shareable for it to be effective.

Pins, unlike Facebook posts or tweets, have a much longer lifespan. Their effects are spread over a period of months. This study found that a full 50% of referral traffic driven by pins takes place after 3.5 months, and 50% of orders happen after 2.5 months.

Moreover, seasonal posts that do well year after year often have Pinterest as their strongest referral channel.

This long lifespan is partly due to the power of the repin. Only 20% of pins are original; the remaining 80% are repins.

If you have a good image that's valuable and relevant to your followers, it's likely that it will be repinned over and over again. In turn, your brand can be exposed to more new potential customers and generate more attention compared to Facebook shares, retweets, and Instagram shares.

That's where the importance of "evergreen" content comes in. Given the long lifespan of a pin, you want to make sure that an image is still relevant a few months down the road if you want people to reSave it.

To create content that not only generates interest but also drives traffic and conversion, make sure your images are themed around your brand message, the culture and conversation you want to create, and the relevance of your products or services. Create boards that give a clear indication of what the images are about so you can attract a highly targeted following who are more likely to repin your images.

And don't forget to do some research. Look at what other pinners and brands are doing in your space to understand what types of images generate the most engagement.

Make Your Pins Go Viral

As you can see above, pins can really have legs if they are valuable, relevant, and share-worthy.

Try these tactics to give more "legs" to your pins:

- "Watermark" your pin by adding your business name and URL to the image.

- Create vertical images as they stand out in Pinterest. A minimum size of 700 px by 800 px is recommended.

- Use catchy titles to garner more repins.

- Rework older posts if necessary to attract more repins.

- Add a Pinterest "Save it" button (formally known as the "Save it" button) to your website to encourage social sharing. You can also explore other plug-ins, such as SumoMe, that offer image share functionality.

- Save (Pin) your images on multiple boards (as long as they're relevant), and set up a schedule to re-pin previous images after a few weeks.

- Join relevant group boards and share your images.

- Don't slack on your alt text. Pinterest pulls an image's alt text as a pin description when someone uses the "Save It" button on your website. Make your alt text descriptive, relevant, and click-worthy.

Generate Excitement and Anticipation

One way to increase sales and conversion is to create buzz and anticipation for new product launches, and you can do that effectively on Pinterest.

Give your followers sneak peeks of what's new and exciting in your product lines. Get them involved in the conversation and maybe even ask for their input about certain features or designs to incorporate into the final product.

You can make this sneak-peek Pinterest-exclusive. Drive traffic from other channels to your Pinterest board to take advantage of the platform's retailer-friendly environment.

Don't forget to pin the link to the product page after the release to make sure your loyal followers who are excited about the buzz can easily purchase the product.

www.tmmpdx.com/top-5-ways-to-build-buzz-with-pinterest

Use the Pinterest "Buy" Button

Pinterest's buyable pins are helping consumers discover new brands, leading to incremental sales for online retailers. Merchants getting a bump are using the social network's pins that let consumers buy products directly within a pin while using the Pinterest mobile app.

business.pinterest.com/en/buyable-pins

Since launching its buy button for iOS devices in June 2015, the number of "buyable pins" has exceeded 60 million. Early results show that buyable pins are "more than doubling" the rate at which shoppers convert into buyers, compared with regular pins. (source)

Pinterest, with its already large collection of "inventory," is evolving from a platform where users browse and then get redirected to external websites into a marketing and discovery platform with ecommerce integrated into the user experience.

Use Pinterest Contest to Generate High-Quality Leads

The use of different boards for different interests allows retailers to attract a highly targeted audience.

Take advantage of this to turn your casual followers into loyal subscribers so you can continue the communication with them through additional channels, such as emails.

One way to do so is to hold a Pinterest contest in which a requirement to join is to opt-in to your mailing list. This generates high-quality leads because they're already expressing interest in your brand.

You can then continue the conversation and warm up your leads by sending newsletters to them with useful information, product updates, and links back to your website.

Here is more information about running Pinterest contests to generate high-quality leads: Social Media Examiner

Measure Your Results

The proof is in the pudding. Any time conversion metrics are involved, you've to look at the data and analytics to gauge the effectiveness of your tactics and make adjustments to maximize the results.

You can use Pinterest's analytics tools to find out how your pins are performing, what people are pinning from your website, who your audience is and how well the "Save it" (formally known as "Save it") buttons are generating referral traffic back to your website.

Pinterest's analytics tool allows you to see how your pins are doing.

You can also get a deeper understanding of your audience by seeing what their interests are so that you can tailor your pins based on their interests.

You can see what other topics your audience is into, and tailor your pins to speak to their interests.

Bonus Tip: Jump on the Video Bandwagon

We all know that video is generating more engagement on social media platforms such as Facebook and Twitter.

Product videos are great tools to drive conversion. Combined with the purchasing mentality of Pinterest users, the use of video represents a great opportunity to drive traffic and increase sales.

At the time of this writing, Pinterest is looking at integrating video and planning on rolling out video ad units. Stay tuned, and make sure you take advantage of the medium when it becomes available on Pinterest.

Pinterest is a fast-evolving platform that can deliver quality exposure, visibility, and quality traffic to your business website or blog. Besides keeping an eye on the latest developments, the best way to get the most out of the platform is to create valuable, relevant, and pinnable content, and then focus on using it to spark conversation, build relationships, and inspire loyalty with your followers.

We caught up with Pinterest power pinner and author Kim Vij, @educatorsspin and asked her to share of her favorite Pinterest PR Secrets. Here they are:

Social PR Secret
Look at interest tabs, play with those words, and see if you can jump into the keywords of your bio, boards, board description, and pin descriptions.

Social PR Secret
Make sure to describe every board in your board description you create, and categorize it. Use key descriptions in your pins, and keep it conversational. Avoid hashtags.

Social PR Secret
What interests your audience? Share third-party content your audience likes, not just your own!

Social PR Secret
Create a secret board while working with a brand or co-partnering with a brand!

Social PR Secret
Schedule your pins out for your campaign. Tool: Tailwind www.tailwindapp.com to schedule pins and bonus it has great analytics!

Social PR Secret
Go for long, vertical pins. Why? Because it shows up better on mobile.

Social PR Secret
Your repins will help you do better in search. Social PR Secret Tip: If someone else has pinned something from my site, I'll pin that from them.

Social PR Secret
What can brands do to optimize their site? Graphics that are pinnable, rich pins on your site.

Social PR Secret
Use warfareplugins.comas a plugin to increase social shares.

Social PR Secret
Use a CTA in your blog posts: "Like it. Save it to Pinterest!"

Social PR Secret
Competitor Research: See what is being pinned from their website, see example URL: www.pinterest.com/source/yourdomain.com

Special thanks to Mike Dane, @Truconversion for contributing to this chapter.

Is Pinterest in Your Best Interest?

Here are a few of Krista Neher's hints to surviving the onslaught of social pictures and pins that are sure to steal your attention (and time!):

- **Content on Pinterest is not time stamped**. Because of this, there's less pressure to post frequently.

- **Use Pinterest as a resource guide.** For example, create a Pinterest board for infographics. Instead of telling your clients to visit your website, direct them to a more precise board with exactly what they're looking for.

- **Use Pinterest as a service.** Krista gives a great example of this: "Make a Pinterest board for events, such as boot camps or meetings, where you can pin the exact location of the hotel along with pictures of what the location looks like."

- **Use "pinnable" images!** Make sure that any images on your blog or website are "pinnable." This will allow greater traffic and more people to share your content if they are interested in it.

You have to Save it to win it.

Chapter 27
LinkedIn PR Secrets: Behind the Blue Velvet Curtain

I always say that *the best ideas come from the most ideas.* When I sat down to write this LinkedIn chapter, filled with some of the best Social PR Secrets for professionals, I called on my favorite sources ranging from those within LinkedIn to those who crack the code from the outside. LinkedIn launched in 2003 and is known as the world's largest and most valuable professional network. At the time of printing of this book, Microsoft announced the acquisition of LinkedIn marking what will surely be a new beginning.

For those about to rock social media and public relations, meet content genius Jason Miller, all the way from the LinkedIn HQ in San Francisco, CA. Jason dropped by @UFSMM (the social media management class I teach at the University of Florida) to give some heavy metal social media tips on how to best optimize your LinkedIn profile!

Off-stage, Jason headlines as the Global Content Marketing Leader for LinkedIn. When he's not ensuring that LinkedIn content is the best it can be, he's snapping photos of rock bands, writing, and promoting his new book. Wow! Can you say, *Superman?*

Jason's new book, *Welcome to the Funnel*, is a combination of everything he's learned from working for Sony and now LinkedIn. I had to ask about all the rock 'n' roll references and, yes, he admitted that he used to play in a heavy metal band—big hair included! He also writes a music blog. His book has no fluff or frills and gets down to the core of how to create content that promotes revenue with a bit of humor and rock star flair.

Unchained: LinkedIn for Business

LinkedIn is now expanding faster than ever. Between where it is today and where it's going, we asked Jason how he thought LinkedIn will expand even more in the years to come.

Jason has been with LinkedIn since 2013 and says that when he got there, his job was to tell the story of the marketer on LinkedIn.

LinkedIn isn't only for finding a job. They've now "positioned themselves to become the definitive professional publishing platform." Users are looking for content: content to inspire them, content to make them better at what they do, content to make them better marketers.

Social PR Secret
"People spend time on other social networks, but invest time in LinkedIn."
– Jason Miller

Behind the Blue Velvet Curtain of LinkedIn Company Pages

We asked Jason some of the tips and tricks to make your LinkedIn profile the best it can be to attract traffic and views.

- **Have a company page.** It's your hub and company identity, so publish content on that page. A company page is crucial to drive traffic back to your site and give viewers an idea of what you're all about.

- **Showcase Pages.** Some companies such as Moz have great showcase pages where you can show off your content.

- **SlideShare.** Some tend to forget that sites like SlideShare aren't just a content repository. SlideShare is a thought leadership platform where you can share your stories in a quick, fun, and visual way.

- **Sponsored Updates.** This is a LinkedIn tool that can take a company update sponsor and target it for brand awareness. If you're trying to reach new viewers, sponsoring a post or blog is a great way to get your name out there!

- **Publishing Platform of LinkedIn Content.** This is one of LinkedIn's newest and most talked-about features. You can publish content on LinkedIn and connect it to your profile or share it with your network. Be proud of your accomplishments and others will take notice.

What Should Your LinkedIn Profile Look Like?

Now that you know more about LinkedIn and the possibilities that come with the network, you have to know some of the do's and don'ts for your very own LinkedIn page. We asked Jason to give us the scoop on both:

- Let's just get the "what not to do" out of the way first by sending you to this blog post that Jason wrote that explains 7 Reasons Your LinkedIn Profile is a Hot Mess.

- Having a good headshot. A professional headshot is one of the first things that people notice. Make sure your picture is sharp.

- Make sure you have a description of yourself and that all sections are filled out.

- Ask for recommendations, even if they aren't your boss. You can even ask professors or someone you've volunteered for.

- Keywords! For business or personal use keywords that are searchable and that describe you, use relative keywords throughout your profile and descriptions. A great example of keyword optimization is the blog Chocolate Donuts by Moz.

- Be yourself and keep your profile open for others to see your content.

Social PR Secret
Write every day and as much as you can using LinkedIn's blog-like, long-form content updates.

So, there you have it, some helpful tips to create, maintain, and expand your LinkedIn profile from the content master himself, Jason Miller!

Next up, I caught up with one of my social media training experts for a look at LinkedIn from the outside. With his picture-perfect LinkedIn profile, Jabez LeBret, Chief Innovation Officer at Get Noticed Get Found (GNGF) and host of the Missing Link Podcat on RainmakerFM, opened up about his most successful Social PR Secrets of optimizing personal LinkedIn profiles to make them stand out. Here's his secret sauce.

Jabez says a complete profile is the most important thing you have on LinkedIn as an incomplete profile may give hiring managers the impression that you're lazy. So keep these 4 P's of LinkedIn profiles in mind while completing your profile!

Follow the 4 P's of LinkedIn Profiles (and it's not P for Perfect).

- Personalize it
- Make it Professional
- Keep up with Progress
- Start Publishing

1. Personalize Your Profile and Background Image

While your qualifications will set you apart, personalizing your profile with an accurately sized background image and professional headshot will make you more memorable.

As far as your profile picture is concerned, the word "professional" doesn't mean it was taken by an award-winning photographer. In this case, it means no selfies, just you in the photo (no cats or arms around friends), just a clean and simple picture so people can see your face. Jabez recommends cropping to no lower than just below your shoulders because, aside from your profile, everywhere else your photo appears on LinkedIn the image is a small thumbnail. And don't forget about the added touch of a background image, the equivalent of other social networks cover image. The background image gives you an even more enhanced way to brand yourself with a dynamic visual.

Social PR Secret
Don't make the mistake of uploading a profile image that is too fun, spammy, random, or sexy. Take off the sunglasses, please. Remember, LinkedIn is the world's largest professional network, not the world's largest cocktail party or sporting event.

2. Make Your Profile Professional

While you can and should represent yourself on LinkedIn, this is not the place to post Instagram photos of your latest meal. Be the person you are in an interview or on the job.

Start with a great headline! Jabez stresses the importance of packing your headline because it follows you around LinkedIn when you participate in discussions and other areas. It's your first marketing touchpoint and gives you the opportunity to tell others who you are before they even click through to your profile. Here's Jabez's beneath his name. Notice how it gives his position, explains what he does, includes a personal factoid and some of his proud accomplishments.

Social PR Secret
Don't say in your headline that you're looking for a job. In fact, don't
say it ever. You're "between opportunities."
– Jabez LeBret

Another hint Jabez dropped to keep your profile professional
was to write your summary in the third person. As he put it,
"Don't write in the first person. Don't sound like an a-hole."
(Thanks for censoring!)

3. Keep Up with Progress

This step is pretty simple, but the hard part is that once you get
behind, it can be hard to catch up. Schedule some time in your
social PR calendar to check on your LinkedIn weekly.

Examine the communities you've joined and look for new ones
that pique your interests. If a community is dying down or you
don't actively participate in it, cut it. More importantly, add new
communities that are very active and cater to your niche. Don't
just join ten and be done with it. Social is a living, breathing
organism and is constantly offering new opportunities.

As you acquire new skills or learn new things on the job, update
your skills section. While the endorsements don't really help you,
they do look good, and you never know when someone will be
searching for a specific skill you have.

Recommendations are where LinkedIn can really help you out.
If hiring managers are looking at various profiles and contacting
leads, they can gain a lot of insight from third-party endorsements.

Try to have at least 5 recommendations to start with.

Recommendations take a while to accumulate, but they will
appear over time. Talk to people you've interned for or with,
classmates with whom you've collaborated on relevant projects,

etc. After you get those five, the best way to keep growing your recommendations is to write them. Most people will return the favor, especially if you reach out to them and ask. Make it a goal to write at least one or two recommendations weekly.

4. Start Publishing on LinkedIn

Jabez claims the LinkedIn publishing platform is the biggest opportunity right now for getting reach, and being an early adopter can only benefit you. And Jabez should know! His article "Why I'm Leaving You Facebook" gave him a lot of insights on the subject that he was wonderful to share with us Publish long-form posts, and you'll see a pencil icon in the share box at the top of your homepage. Brands can't publish yet, but individuals can and should interact with the platform to get exposure, followers, and build relationships.

The Facebook breakup letter was Jabez's first published piece on LinkedIn and explains how he is fed up with Facebook as a personal user constantly being tested on. And what better way to say "I'm out of here Facebook" than on LinkedIn!

Here's what he learned:

- He had 4,000 views and 400 shares, giving him a share rate of 10%—not bad.

- His followers grew from 2 to nearly 3,000 with just one article! So 75% of people who read that article followed him.

This success rate may be hard to duplicate with every article, but if you have great content that people are interested in, there's no telling how far publishing on LinkedIn can take you.

There you have it, the 4 P's of building a stand-out LinkedIn profile and the benefits of self-publishing on LinkedIn. I hope all of Jabez's LinkedIn insights have inspired you to login and make some changes today! Don't worry if you forgot your password, there's a retrieval system.

Happy updating!

Recruit. Culture. News: Meet Your LinkedIn Company Page

After optimizing your LinkedIn profile page, it's time to create your LinkedIn company page. Such pages work best for companies with multiple employees. They give a great respect to your company and highlight the profile of all your employees.

For instance, HubPage has created a huge fan following of 16,500 followers with their LinkedIn company page. The page has also resulted in the creation of a group with over 82,000 members. As a result, their conversion rate stands at 2.7%, which is 3 times higher than for Facebook or Twitter.

However, having a company page does not only boost your conversions, but also helps recruiters save a ton of money.

Let's take a look at this example below:

Schawk, a leading global brand production and deployment firm, has saved over $200k in recruiting costs and has saved considerable time in the process.

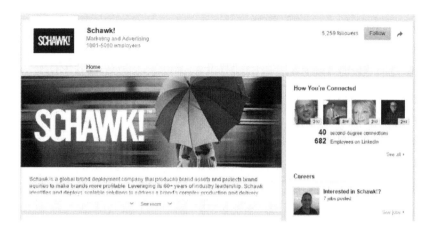

Your company page is a meeting avenue for people interested in your business and serves larger business better than solopreneurs.

To assist you to create the perfect LinkedIn profile, check out this infographic by TruConversion.

Remember: There's no single rule to create a perfect LinkedIn profile or LinkedIn Company Page. Take a note of the basics, and derive maximum benefit from the features and you're one step ahead of the game.

Chapter contributors: Mike Dane and Sydney Thompson

Chapter 28
Twitter Social #PR Secrets Report News, Gain Publicity, & Build Relationships

Twitter is more than just a social media darling that soared onto the New York Stock Exchange under the symbol #TWTR (on.wsj.com/Vmry3W). The micro-blogging social network can be one of the quickest and most effective ways to share your brand's news and engage your audience.

Let's look at the Tweets stats: Twitter boasts 320 million active users with over 1 billion unique visits monthly to sites with embedded tweets. They are talking (and listening) about everything from mobile apps to cars to scientific breakthroughs to news, and of course businesses and brands.

140 Character Press Release

Less than five years ago, press releases were the main go-to strategy to share company news and get the word out to journalists, customers, investors, prospects and search engines. Today, we have an almost dizzying choice of ways to spread social news,

with Twitter being one of the leading ways to share 140-charac-
ter news Tweets and score social authority and influence on an
industry or subject matter.

6 Ways to Raise Your Social PR Stock with Twitter

1. Play Hearts: Want to get someone's attention on Twitter? Like
one of their tweets with a click of a heart! It sends a nice message
and will make you stand out in the crowd. The act of "liking" can
be a less public way to grab a blogger's attention or get noticed by
a person of interest. The Twitter (blog.twitter.com/2015/hearts-
on-twitter) feature that was updated in November 2015 allows
users to "like" a Tweet by clicking on a small heart (previously a
star" icon on the Tweets they find amusing or useful. Doing so
both bookmarks the tweet and alerts its creator that they appre-
ciate the sentiment without republishing it in their own streams.

2. Visual Storytelling on Twitter: Move over Instagram. Until
now, seeing an image attached to a Tweet has required tapping on
a link, leaving Twitter out of step with visual social networks like
Facebook, Tumblr, and Instagram. That change began with last
month's update that inserts previews of images and Vines (blog.
twitter.com/2013/picture-this-more-visual-tweets) directly into
tweets. What can you do with this from a Social PR standpoint?
A strong storytelling visual as part of your Tweet can catch the
eye of that researching journalist looking for story ideas and
sources on Twitter.

3. Get Your Story Carded with Twitter Cards (dev.twitter.com/
docs/cards)**:** Maximize your news story potential using Twitter
cards (a few lines of HTML meta tags) to attract a social reader
and gain more publicity and visibility. Twitter cards are a way
to display extra information that goes beyond the 140-character
limit Twitter imposes. For example, here's what a Twitter card
for a recent Fast Company article looks like:

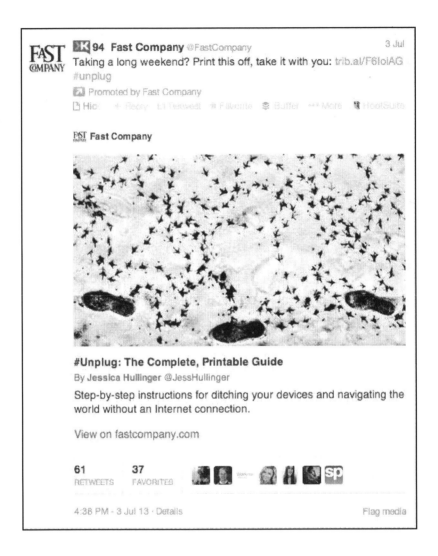

4. Twitter profile optimization for media: How many characters does your bio have? Link to the news section of your website
versus the homepage. Make it easy for media on Twitter to find
your latest company news. Optimize the experience for the journalists and bloggers who are most likely to click on that link and
send them to the news area of your website.

5. Twitter Timing is Everything: Let's face it, social media is time-consuming and can easily result in lost productivity, effort, and resources. Getting the most visibility, publicity, and exposure is key with any social media network, so take timing into consideration to maximize leverage.

Timing can make a difference and Dan Zarrella studied timing in his recent book, *The Science of Marketing*. He reported that:

- Tweeting later in the day gets a higher click-through rate than mornings.

- End of the week tweets get more clicks than Monday to Wednesday tweets.

- Weekends are made for tweeting and get higher CTR - tweet it out and see.

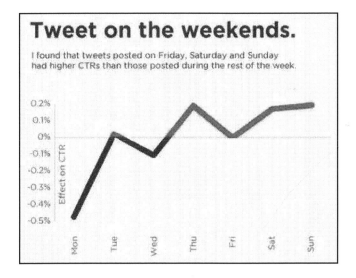

Timeout: The Twitter timing gospel this is definitely not. If anything, use Zarrella's findings as a starting point or inspiration to see the times that work best for your brand's Twitter news stream.

6. Hot Twitter Apps and Platforms: Making our lives easier and creating a better content experience for our followers—isn't that what we strive for? Okay, so maybe not in that order, but both are important.

- Followerwonk (followerwonk.com): If social growth is your focus, this Moz app is worth checking out. With a free version, there are no excuses and all wins. Followerwonk helps explore and grow your social graph with Twitter analytics to find, optimize, and analyze for maximum social growth

- Twitterfeed (twitterfeed.com): Part of the bitly family, this free tool makes it a no-brainer to tweet the last posts published in a blog via the RSS feed.

- Buffer (bufferapp.com/app): You're new Twitter content strategy friend! Buffer makes it super easy to automagically share posts for you through the day.

- GIF Party: How did Twitter get the word out in early March 2016 that they now had GIFs? Well, what better way to share a GIF than to have a worldwide #GIFParty on Twitter and everyone was invited (twitter.com/twitter/status/705422500465803264/photo/1.) Sharing a GIF can say the words to in animated form.

- Twitter Poll – Polling isn't just for politicians, it's for social media managers and PR pros like you! Ask a question about a new product, to finish a sentence, or ask what makes them happy: a grumpy cat or a fluffy dog. These are just some ways to get your audience engaged and interactive.

Twitter PR Tips to Increase Media Coverage

- Make sure to announce news on Twitter at the same time as other company news channels.

- Keep your company's online newsroom Twitter-friendly and up-to-date with fresh content (and an easy way to share straight from your site with a catchy headline, hashtag and a username!)

- Have an easy landing page showcasing your Twitter stream for easy access.

- Create a Twitter account specifically for your company news and automatically publish all content from your online newsroom. You'll reach one in 10 journalists that way!

- Upload an image, search for a GIF, or create a video with a news tweet to stand out in the Twitter feed.

- Optimize news with *relative* trending hashtags.

- Avoid abusive hashtag hijacking, which is using a hashtag in a tweet that has no relation to the hashtag subject. Beware: this can seriously backfire and potentially cause severe reputation management problems.

- If you haven't already done so, start monitoring activity via a platform such as Tweetdeck, a a cool and efficient way to monitor what journalists you care about are writing and sharing.

- Be selfless and helpful. Interact with the media when you don't need them by liking some of their tweets, giving them congrats on a success, or sharing information they might be interested in that has nothing to do with you.

Getting the most out of Twitter without Twitter getting the most out of you is a daily challenge for consumers, journalists, media, and brands both small and large. Following Twitter best practices can ease the pain and increase the exposure rate.

It's no secret, the tweet goes on with or without you.

Whether you follow hashtags or cashtags (bit.ly/1oNnzd0) on Twitter, make sure your Twitter messaging is optimized with the media in mind.

Chapter 29
Namaste Sane: Space and Mindfulness in Your Social PR Life

"I wish I had more social media in my life," said nobody ever.

My social media life mantra is simple: create more space for opportunity. This might seem obvious, but it takes work and being able to take a step on the outside of what's holding you back.

Did you ever have an "aha" moment? Mine came to me after I wrote the first edition of *Social PR Secrets*. Once my business coach convinced me to actually *start* writing, I finished the bulk of the manuscript in less than three months! It was amazing. How did I complete it so quickly, especially since it took me a year to get from the chapter outline to writing Chapter One?

Social PR Secret
The hardest part is getting started. Just hit the start button, and things get easier.

Spaceful Schedules

Working in the social media world can be more than distracting—it can easily sabotage the best of agendas, projects, and intentions!

For example, to get me started on *Social PR Secrets*, there was business planning I had to do in order to get myself off projects, transition staff to cover for me, and delegate or say "no" to new opportunities. What? How do you do that?

My coach, Charlie Gilkey of Productive Flourishing, put me on a strictly "spaced" schedule: every Monday, Wednesday, and Friday I'd start my day with a yoga class from 9:00 to 10:30. Then, I would immediately go to the closest coffee shop with my laptop and start writing—no calls, no email, no social media sneaks, etc. I'd write for about two or three hours, and then head back to my office to answer any emails and tie up loose ends for the day.

At first, I thought he was crazy, but I gave it a try. Before I knew it, my book was done!

It all seemed to flow from down dog to up dog and out of my brain, and through my typing fingertips.

Social PR Secret
Create space for creativity and focus to flourish.

What I realized is that I not only created space in my schedule for something I didn't think I had time for, but I created space for creativity and focus to flourish. One of the many benefits of yoga is that it allows the creative juices to start flowing when your mind and body release the mental blocks. All of those deep breaths reset your mind back to its natural state—calm, focused, and sharp.

All of a sudden, I felt like I had three times the space in my brain, resulting in a recipe for #SocialPRSuccess.

Social Media is Calling

Let's face it: social media takes up a lot of space in our lives. If you work in the social media marketing world, the need for detox (or alcohol!) is almost inevitable. Whether it's for our personal or professional lives, social media is a space—and time-sucker. It's an endless task of reading, writing, posting, creating visuals, captioning, tagging, filtering, cropping, chatting, sharing, commenting, and don't forget the trusty old email inbox! With all of this to do, who has time for anything else?

So, how can we create more space in our lives to actually make time outside of the newsfeed and away from our mobile devices? Since we can't just buy more memory or storage and our brains don't come with an upgrade option, we're on our own to create more space for the things—like health, family, friends, vacations—that are most important to us.

Below is a list of things I'm doing to create more space in my life for what I love and also to make me better at what I'm already doing.

Upgrade Your Memory

Today, I upgraded my computer to the maximum amount of memory it'll take to speed things up and save time. (I even installed it myself, although I wouldn't recommend that because it would save time and frustration to hire a professional.) On any given work day, I have more than 20 tabs open in multiple windows in three browsers. If you work in the social media, PR, or journalism worlds, I'm sure you can relate.

I also call and video conference with Skype and use Google HOA for chat and calls. Adding memory to my computer has already helped speed things up. Ultimately, this will create more space in my life in the form of time.

Action item: Check how much memory your computer has and see if it can be upgraded. It's a cheap way to gain more speed.

Clear Your Clutter

Desk Space

I'm constantly cleaning off my desk space to remove as much clutter as possible and only keep what I absolutely need for what I'm working on in that minute. It helps me stay focused and eliminates visual distractions and reminders of other things that I could be doing.

Action item: Clear off your desktop every day before and after work.

Desktop/Laptop Space

I'll confess that I have a bad habit of saving lots of things to my computer's desktop. This sucks up computer speed and memory, in addition to being a visual reminder of disorganization. I have a schedule to clear out the space by saving it all to an external hard drive, in case I ever need it. (Baby steps!) I've also created files in Dropbox and I'm starting to wean myself away from using the desktop as one big filing cabinet.

Action item: On your computer, create folders and subfolders and organize icons so the ones you use the most are the easiest to access.

Closet Space

Three piles: keep, donate, or sell. If you haven't worn it in the past six months and can't say "I love this!" then it's not a keeper. Love it or leave it. That cluttered closet is haunting you at your most creative moments. It's like a haunted closet turning you into a zombie who thinks they need to first clean out the closet before they can start _____. Mine is usually writing an article or a chapter in this book.

I cleared out about 75% of the clothes in my closet and put them in my garage. (More baby steps!) I have a homeless charity come by a few times a year. This might not seem like something related to work life, but it actually is a very liberating.

Action item: Only save it if you love it.

Desk, computer, or office clutter: It's all clutter, and it impacts your brain. Princeton University researchers found that physical clutter in your surroundings competes for your attention, resulting in decreased performance and increased stress.

Boost Your Brain

Meditation for Business and Life Strategy

Until about six months ago, the most meditation I did came at the end of a yoga class. Although it was always my favorite part, I never really looked at it as if I was practicing meditation. But then I saw the image below on Instagram of your brain before and after a 10-minute meditation and thought, *Wow!* It made sense to me because I walk into a yoga class as one person and walk out as a new-and-improved being, ready to embrace and conquer the world again.

In a weird, serendipitous way, one day later, I came across an article in Marie Claire talking about how women are using mediation as a business strategy and how it gives them an upper hand in negotiating and communicating to get what they want. Interesting, right? So, I looked into this even more and found this article on how meditation is massively powerful.

Meditation:

- Influences weight control

- Reduces anxiety

- Increases empathy and compassion

- Improves memory function

Meditation can help us all to be more rational, creative, mindful, and likable people. Sign me up!

Social PR Secret

Want to add calmness, clarity and creativity to your social media day? Download Buddhify app today and thank me later, it's the key to modern day mindfulness. This award-winning mindfulness app has over 80 guided meditations custom-made for wherever you are and whatever you're doing—traveling, at work, at home, going to sleep and much more.

Get Up, Get Out, and Turn it Upside-Down

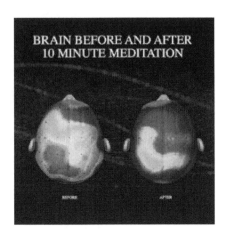

You've probably heard them all a million times: take a walk during work, don't sit at a computer all day, take breaks to restore and rejuvenate, etc. It's hard to do and easy to hit the snooze on taking breaks. Trust me, I, unfortunately, specialize in workaholism. The only thing that keeps me honest is my Fitbit, but it's super hard to get up and do something during working hours. I'm always scrambling at the end of the day because of how many steps I need to reach in order to prevent feeling as though I'm wasting my humanity.

What's the cost of not doing it? I schedule stuff that will cost me if I cancel. Many times, I schedule a Pilates class during lunch and about one hour before I think to myself, "This is a huge mistake. What in the world was I thinking? I have so much to do! Cancel, cancel, cancel!"

But, since I pay in advance for the class, I go. It's always totally worth it, and here's why: one hour later, I sit back at my computer for a TwitterChat or something where I need to be all brain parts in full throttle. All of a sudden, my thoughts are crystal-clear and my creativity oozes out.

Here's an unsolicited Tweet I received after attending a Twitter-Chat that followed my Pilates/meditation class. After, I received this message, Andy Crestodina, industry expert and author of Content Chemistry, who was a guest on the chat, wrote:

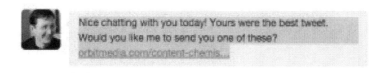

Cool Part #1: He complimented my tweets and offered to send me one of his books.

Cool Part #2: I then asked him to be a guest for my University of Florida Social Media Management class. He said yes! I give the credit for all of this to that lunchtime Pilates class. It pulled me out of my delirious funk of staring at the Facebook newsfeed and stimulated the space in my brain to improve my communication skills.

Social PR Secret
You can replace Pilates with walking around the block or office a few times or doing laps around the mall, down the street, etc.

Handstands

Social media has a way of turning your world upside-down—for the good and bad. Why not fight fire with fire? I add a few handstands to my week, and it's good to know that there are more benefits to handstands than just the physical ones. Handstands can actually make you feel happier. As the blood flows to your brain, it has an energizing and calming effect, especially when you're feeling stressed out. Handstands can also give you a mood makeover because they help reduce the production of cortisol, a stress hormone. The magic of handstands won't only de-stress you in the short-term, but it could also help relieve minor depression and anxiety over the long-haul.

If you find space in your life to function and flourish, every little thing will be all right. Don't worry about a thing!

#NamaStaySane

Chapter 30
Social PR Wisdom

In my social PR journey, many people have inspired me along the way. From the best bosses to the most frustrating to some of the most powerful and passionate CEOs, authors, speakers, clients, friends, mentors, "frenemies," experts, consultants, business coaches, personal trainers, yoga instructors, doctors, journalists, and—most recently—the search marketing and social media industry.

One standout social PR inspiration I encountered early on was Tony Hsieh, CEO of Zappos.com, Inc. and author of *Delivering Happiness: A Path to Profits, Passion, and Purpose* (amzn. to/1rs2sLF). An early adopter of Twitter, he flocked to social media as a path to share his inspirations, in addition to learning how to cultivate a culture of happiness and success through his wins and losses.

I am happy to share my journals, sticky notes, and excerpts from my social PR life.

Un-Friend Your Fears

The PR industry during the millennium, dot-com, go-go days was an interesting time, especially with emerging technology startups. Checks were being FedExed to my agency, without proposals, from companies I'd never spoken to. One of my dot-com clients was a CEO trying to raise money to go public. We were planning media tours and investor road shows with the big shots on Wall Street, Madison Avenue, and Silicon Valley.

One social PR secret I had to keep for my client was the fact he was gay. At the time being *out* was not *in*. It was a different era when the good old boys on Wall Street would not accept homosexuality on a term sheet and might actually blacklist someone for something along those lines. Coming out of the gate and being the first to do something or get labeled means risking it all for the reward of someone in the future. Today, same-sex marriage is one of the most talked-about topics on Twitter and in blogs, and being gay on Wall Street is now just a blip on the social radar. Being *authentic* is in.

Today's public is looking to have a transparent and meaningful relationship with brands. These days it's less about contrived messaging and more about being real, even if real means tripping and getting back up, making mistakes and owning up to it, closing chapters and starting new ones, and sometimes turning everything off and reinventing your brand or yourself from the bottom up.

More has changed in public relations and the media in the past five years than in the past 100 years, so the social PR soul searching is really just beginning.

The Best Seat in the House for Opportunity

I've spent the last 10 years speaking at leading Internet marketing conferences on the subject matter of social media and SEO as it relates to public relations. Webinars, conferences, workshops, and online training courses are a new way of life for me, and I love sharing the perspective of how PR plays into the game. But what I love even more than speaking is the opportunity to attend the other sessions at a conference.

I map out my session plan ahead of time, and I always sit in the front row with my laptop or iPad, feverishly taking notes. Sitting in the front row gives you the advantage of having less distractions, more focus, and a better networking opportunity because most of the other front-runners are live bloggers or members of the media who are there to cover the session. Some of my best contacts and relationships have either been made sitting in the front row or in the speaker room at a conference.

From #Fail to #Success

Besides staying in the news with a positive angle, part of the daily routine of a social PR professional is to stay ahead of the news, reading all of the relative buzz surrounding your brand's industry and the world events that impact everyone. But, when the cringing moment comes and you read a negative story about your brand, client, or yourself in the media, all the good fades to nausea.

One of my favorite employees who had the ultimate and, of course, authentic British accent, Radley Moss, was called out in a print story by the editor of a Florida business journal. The headline, "Some Pitches are in the Dirt," called our story idea "Internet hype." Radley brought the article into my office and read it to me. I said, "Call the editor up and ask him to lunch." So the three of us met for lunch, and from that experience we gained some valuable advice from the editor about how and what to pitch, and the editor also got to hear what life was like on our side of the media fence. The failures are what make us stronger and give us opportunities to grow and succeed.

These days in our social media world, the opportunity to fail is at an all-time high for a publicist of any sort—business or celebrity. One wrong move by anyone within a company ends up in the lap of the PR department.

Keep Moving With the PR Cheese

It would be easy if the same old routines always worked in every situation. In the book, *Who Moved My Cheese: An Amazing Way to Deal With Change in Your Work and in Your Life* (amzn. to/ZvtA4A) by Spencer Johnson, the characters are faced with unexpected change. Just as in the digital marketing, media, and PR industries, dealing with change is like a maze.

Social PR Secret
Once you realize that failing doesn't mean that it's the end of the world, changing becomes a little easier.

Staying in the same PR routine for more than a few years is old cheese. Being flexible, keeping things simple, and giving yourself the green light to move quickly allows you the space to notice that when a situation changes, you should change with it. Social media has caused more than change for PR; it has caused an enormous opportunity shift. The University of Florida College of Journalism now offers an Online Master of Arts in Communication (socialmediadegree.jou.ufl.edu) with a specialization in Social Media that is worth checking out.

Social PR Secret
"The only thing you can change is how you relate or how you react to something." – Chelsea Dipaola, Guruv Yoga instructor

Social publicist and digital strategist Lisa Grimm puts it like this: "Don't accept the structures around you. Pick something small, build something new, and get results so you can build more new things."

Social PR Secret
Don't sit around and think how you can be like other people, brands, or companies. Define your own way, your own structure for operating, and the creative processes that drive your purpose and objectives.

The new social PR cheese comes full of opportunity. Take a bite, keep moving, and create the space for things to happen.

About the Author

*"That's why it's called a practice. We have to practice
a practice if it is to be of value."*
—Allan Lokos, (bit.ly/Y5xL6t) Patience:
The Art of Peaceful Living (amzn.to/1kBUn8s)

When it comes to balancing relationships, Lisa Buyer
(@lisabuyer (twitter.com/lisabuyer)) believes the practice
of public relations, social media, and SEO is exponential. As the
founder of three PR agencies and CEO of The Buyer Group
(www.thebuyergroup.com), Lisa is ambitious about the influence of public relations on social media, SEO, and SEM, and
she continues to share her innovative approach with her followers, clients, peers, and associates. Heading her current boutique
agency, The Buyer Group, Lisa consults on both the client side
and agency side.

You can find Lisa on the faculty directory for the University of
Florida College of Journalism where she teaches Social Media
Management to public relations students. She's been published
in Mashable, has written and tweeted for industry publications
Search Engine Watch (bit.ly/1sW417q) and ClickZ (www.
clickz.com) and she is the editor of her own online publication,

SocialPRChat.com. Lisa is often recognized for her inspirational and motivational style. She is an educator and a frequent speaker at search and social conferences, workshops, and webinars, globally. She is an unofficial brand advocate for @Canva, @Buffer, @HaikuDeck, and @Buddhify.

Lisa helps clients connect the social media and PR dots while also educating agencies transitioning from traditional media to today's best digital strategies. Past clients include public and private companies in the technology, real estate, banking, and health/beauty industries as well as marketing and advertising agencies.

She is a regular speaker and moderator on topics of online PR, social media, and search at national conferences including ClickZ Live, SMX, Social Pro, Pubcon, PRSSA, and Media-Post. She is a graduate of the University of Florida with a degree in Public Relations and Business Administration. (Go Gators!) (gatorzone.com)

Lisa lives in Celebration, Florida with her family: Don, Kennedy, Audrey, and Grant. Besides #SocialPR, Lisa's favorite hashtags include #yoga, #surf, and #sunsets.

"Practice and all is coming."
—Sri K. Pattabhi Jois

Hear Lisa Speak

Lisa Buyer is available as a keynote speaker or panelist to create a Social PR presentation for your organization, conference, or special event.

She can travel to you or deliver a presentation via a webinar.

You can also see the schedule of various conferences and events that Lisa will be speaking at here:
thebuyergroup.com/speaking/

To schedule an event or training or inquire about consulting services with Lisa Buyer, contact her directly at:
Namaste@thebuyergroup.com

What's next?

Lisa is currently writing her next book:

#Space to Live. Work. Love.
How to create space in your life for success and opportunity

#SocialPRSecrets Twitter List

twitter.com/TheBuyerGroup/lists/socialprsecrets

123rf.com
@123rf
twitter.com/123rf

21 Habit
@21habit
twitter.com/21habit

Adam Singer
@adamsinger
twitter.com/AdamSinger

Adblade
@OfficialAdblade
twitter.com/OfficialAdblade

Trapit (Formerly known as Addvocate)
@Trapit
twitter.com/trapit

AG Jeans
@agjeans
twitter.com/AGJeans

aimClear
@aimClear
twitter.com/aimclear

Amy Vernon
@amyvernon
twitter.com/amyvernon

Angie Schottmuller
@aschottmuller
twitter.com/aschottmuller

AP
@ap
twitter.com/AP

Blitzmetrics.com
@BlitzMetrics
twitter.com/BlitzMetrics

Blogger
@Blogger
twitter.com/Blogger

Boot Camp Digital
@bootcampdigital
twitter.com/bootcampdigital

Bruce Clay Inc
@BruceClayInc
twitter.com/BruceClayInc

Buffer App
@buffer
twitter.com/buffer

Business Wire
@businesswire
twitter.com/BusinessWire

BuzzStream
@buzzstream
twitter.com/buzzstream

BuzzSumo
@BuzzSumo
twitter.com/BuzzSumo

Camera+
@taptaptap
twitter.com/taptaptap

Canva
@Canva
twitter.com/canva

Catherine Rampell
@crampell
twitter.com/crampell

Cathy Hackl
@CathyHackl
https://twitter.com/CathyHackl

Charlie Gilkey
@CharlieGilkey
twitter.com/CharlieGilkey

Chat Salad
@chatsalad
twitter.com/chatsalad

Chelsea Adams
@ChelseaBeaAdams
twitter.com/ChelseaBeaAdams

Chris Brogan
@chrisbrogan
twitter.com/chrisbrogan

Cision
@cision
twitter.com/cision

ClearVoice
@ClearVoice
twitter.com/ClearVoice

ClickZ
@ClickZ
twitter.com/ClickZ

ClickZ Live
@clickzlive
twitter.com/clickzlive

ClickZ Academy
@incisive
twitter.com/incisive

CNN
@cnn
twitter.com/CNN

ContentDJ
@contentdjapp
twitter.com/contentdjapp

CopyBlogger
@copyblogger
twitter.com/copyblogger

Dan Zarrella
@danzarrella
twitter.com/danzarrella

Dana Todd
@DanaTodd
twitter.com/danatodd

Danny Sullivan
@DannySullivan
twitter.com/dannysullivan

Danny Whatmough
@DannyWhatmough
twitter.com/DannyWhatmough

David McInnis
@giantcranberry
twitter.com/giantcranberry

David Meerman Scott
@DMScott
twitter.com/dmscott

Dennis Yu
@dennisyu
twitter.com/dennisyu

Digg
@Digg
twitter.com/digg

Dropbox
@dropbox
twitter.com/Dropbox

DudaMobile
@dudamobile
twitter.com/DudaMobile

e-Releases
@ereleases
twitter.com/ereleases

Edelman Trust Barometer
@edelmanpr
twitter.com/edelmanpr

Ekaterina Walter
@ekaterina
twitter.com/ekaterina

Facebook
@Facebook
twitter.com/facebook

Fast Company
@FastCompany
twitter.com/FastCompany

Followerwonk
@Followerwonk
twitter.com/followerwonk

GetRealChat
@PamMktgNut
twitter.com/PamMktgNut

Google
@Google
twitter.com/google

Gorkana
@Gorkana
twitter.com/Gorkana

Greg Jarboe
@gregjarboe
twitter.com/gregjarboe

Gneo Day
@gneoday
twitter.com/gneoday

Guruv Yoga
@tymihoward
twitter.com/tymihoward

Guy Kawasaki
@GuyKawasaki
twitter.com/GuyKawasaki

Haiku Deck
@HaikuDeck
twitter.com/HaikuDeck

HARO
@haro
twitter.com/helpareporter

Hashtracking.com
@hashtracking
twitter.com/Hashtracking

Heidi Cohen
@heidicohen
twitter.com/heidicohen

Heyo
@heyo
twitter.com/heyo

Hitwise
@experianmkt
twitter.com/experianmkt

Hootsuite
@hootsuite
twitter.com/hootsuite

HubSpot
@hubspot
twitter.com/HubSpot

Huffpost Live
@huffpostlive
twitter.com/HuffPostLive

Ian Cleary
@IanCleary
twitter.com/IanCleary

If This Then That
@IFTTT
twitter.com/IFTTT

Infogr.am
@infogram
twitter.com/infogram

Inkybee
@TheInkyBee
twitter.com/TheInkybee

Instagram
@instagram
twitter.com/instagram

Instant E-Training
@IETraining
twitter.com/IETraining

Instaquote
@getinstaquote
twitter.com/getinstaquote

Jabez LeBret
@jabezlebret
twitter.com/jabezlebret

Jason Kintzler
@jasonkintzler
twitter.com/jasonkintzler

Jennine Miller
@JennineMiller
twitter.com/jenninemiller

Jesse Thomas
@jessethomas
twitter.com/jessethomas

JETLAUNCH
@jetlaunchllc
twitter.com/jetlaunchllc

Joanna Lord
@JoannaLord
twitter.com/JoannaLord

Joe Laratro
@jlaratro
twitter.com/jlaratro

Julie Talenfield
@boardroompr
twitter.com/boardroompr

Kim Vij
@EducatorsSpin
twitter.com/educatorsspin

Klout
@klout
twitter.com/klout

Kred
@kred
twitter.com/Kred

Krista Neher
@kristaneher
twitter.com/KristaNeher

Kristi Kellogg
@KristiKellogg
twitter.com/KristiKellogg

La Gondola Chicago
@lagondola
twitter.com/LaGondola

Lab42
@Lab42Research
twitter.com/Lab42Research

Larry Kim
@LarryKim
https://twitter.com/larrykim

Lauren Donovan
@beebow
twitter.com/beebow

Lee Odden
@leeodden
twitter.com/leeodden

LexisNexis
@LexisNexis
twitter.com/LexisNexis

Lisa Grimm
@lulugrimm
twitter.com/lulugrimm

Lisa Williams
@SEOPollyAnna
twitter.com/SEOPollyAnna

Lululemon
@lululemon
twitter.com/lululemon

Malcolm Gladwell
@gladwell
twitter.com/Gladwell

Marketwired
@marketwired
twitter.com/marketwired

Marty Weintrub
@aimclear
twitter.com/aimclear

Mashable
@mashable
twitter.com/mashable

Matt McGowan
@matt_mcgowan
twitter.com/matt_mcgowan

Medium
@Medium
twitter.com/Medium

Melanie Mitchell
@MelanieMitchell
twitter.com/MelanieMitchell

Mel Carson
@melcarson
twitter.com/melcarson

Melissa Fach
@SEOAware
https://twitter.com/SEOAware

Meltwater
@Meltwater
twitter.com/Meltwater

mention
@mention
twitter.com/mention

Michell Marie
@imizze
twitter.com/imizze

Mike Volp
@mvolpe
twitter.com/mvolpe

Moz
@Moz
twitter.com/Moz

MSNBC
@MSNBC
twitter.com/msnbc

MuckRack
@muckrack
twitter.com/muckrack

My News Desk
@mynewsdesk
twitter.com/mynewsdesk

Navah Berg
@Navahk
twitter.com/navahk

Neal Schaffer
@NealSchaffer
twitter.com/NealSchaffer

New York Times
@nytimes
twitter.com/nytimes

Nick Cicero
@NickCicero
https://twitter.com/nickcicero

Newsvine
@Newsvine
twitter.com/newsvine

Nordstrom
@nordstrom
twitter.com/nordstrom

Outbrain
@Outbrain
twitter.com/Outbrain

Paper.li
@Paper_li
twitter.com/Paper_li

Paula Allen
@paulaspeak
twitter.com/paulaspeak

Brandwatch React (Formerly Known As PeerIndex)
@BW_React
twitter.com/BW_React

Peg Fitzpatrick
@PegFitzpatrick
twitter.com/pegfitzpatrick

Peter Bregman
@peterbregman
twitter.com/peterbregman

Peter Shankman
@PeterShankman
twitter.com/petershankman

PicMonkey
@pikmonkeyapp
twitter.com/PicMonkeyApp

PiktoChart
@piktochart
twitter.com/piktochart

Pinterest
@pinterest
twitter.com/pinterest

PitchEngine
@pitchengine
twitter.com/pitchengine

Pluggio
@pluggio
twitter.com/pluggio

PressFeed
@pressfeed
twitter.com/PRESSfeed

PRNewswire
@prnewswire
twitter.com/PRNewswire

ProfNet
@ProfNet
twitter.com/ProfNet

PRWeb
@PRWeb
twitter.com/prweb

Pubcon
@pubcon
twitter.com/pubcon

Quantcast
@Quantcast
twitter.com/Quantcast

Rafflecopter
@Rafflecopter
twitter.com/rafflecopter

Rand Fishkin
@randfish
twitter.com/randfish

Razor Social
@RazorSocial
https://twitter.com/razorsocial

Rebecca Murtagh
@virtualmarketer
twitter.com/virtualmarketer

RebelMouse
@rebelmouse
twitter.com/rebelmouse

Reddit
@reddit
twitter.com/reddit

Reuters
@Reuters
twitter.com/Reuters

Rite Tag
@RiteTag
twitter.com/RiteTag

Roy Oppenheim
@oplaw
twitter.com/OPlaw

Salesforce
@Salesforce
twitter.com/salesforce

Sarah Evans
@prsarahevans
twitter.com/prsarahevans

Sarah Van Elzen
@SarahVanElzen
twitter.com/SarahVanElzen

Seek or Shout
@SeekOrShout
twitter.com/SeekOrShout

Scoop It
@scoopit
twitter.com/scoopit

Scribe
@ScribeContent
twitter.com/ScribeContent

Search Engine Watch
@sewatch
twitter.com/sewatch

Search Engine Marketing Professional Organization (SEMPO)
@sempoglobal
twitter.com/sempoglobal

Shelly Kramer
@ShellyKramer
twitter.com/ShellyKramer

SimplyMeasured
@simplymeasured
twitter.com/simplymeasured

Search Marketing Expo (SMX)
@smx
twitter.com/smx

Snapchat
@Snapchat
twitter.com/snapchat

Social Mention
@socialmention
twitter.com/socialmention

Starbucks
@starbucks
twitter.com/starbucks

StumbleUpon
@stumbleupon
twitter.com/StumbleUpon

Suzanne Somers
@SuzanneSomers
twitter.com/SuzanneSomers

Sway Group
@SwayGroup
https://twitter.com/SwayGroup

Sydney Renee Thompson
@SydneyRThompson
twitter.com/SydneyRThompson

Taboola
@Taboola
twitter.com/taboola

TechCrunch
@techcrunch
twitter.com/TechCrunch

TEKGroup
@tekgroup
twitter.com/TEKGROUP

The Buyer Group
@thebuyergroup
twitter.com/thebuyergroup

The Next Web
@TheNextWeb
twitter.com/TheNextWeb

The Wall Street Journal
@WSJ
twitter.com/WSJ

Tony Hsieh
@zappos
twitter.com/zappos

Triberr
@triberr
twitter.com/Triberr

Tweetdeck
@tweetdeck
twitter.com/TweetDeck

Twitter
@Twitter
twitter.com/twitter

University of Florida College of Journalism
@UFJSchool
twitter.com/@UFJSchool

University of Florida Social Media Management Class
@UFSMM
twitter.com/UFSMM

USAToday
@USATODAY
twitter.com/USATODAY

Vine
@vineapp
twitter.com/vineapp

Virginia Nussey
@VirginiaNussey
twitter.com/VirginiaNussey

Visual.ly
@visually
twitter.com/Visually

Cision (Formerly known as Vocus)
@Cision
twitter.com/Cision

Walmart
@walmart
twitter.com/walmart

WEBSTA
@websta_me
twitter.com/websta_me

Whole Foods
@Wholefoods
twitter.com/WholeFoods

Wildfire
@wildfireapp
twitter.com/wildfireapp

WooBox
@woobox
twitter.com/woobox

YouTube
@youtube
twitter.com/YouTube

Social PR Secret
Want to know how to alphabetize a long list in 5 seconds?
alphabetizer.flap.tv/

Glossary
Your Social PR Terminology Cheat Sheet

Activity by Day: How a brand's responsiveness (on average) changes over the course of a week.

Activity by Hour: How a brand's responsiveness (on average) changes over the course of a day.

Amplification: The way in which, through audience engagement, a piece of content reaches the secondary and tertiary (and on) levels of a brand's social presence. This can vary by channel, RTs on Twitter, Shares on FB, Shares on G+, Regram on Instagram, Repins on Pinterest, but the goal is the same.

Analytics: Processes and technologies that enable social media marketers and public relations pros to evaluate the success of their Social PR marketing initiatives by measuring performance.

Attribution: Tracking and understanding what campaigns on which channels are responsible for a brand's social media successes and failures.

Audience Growth: The rate at which a brand adds (or loses) audience members.

- Facebook – Fans or Likes
- Twitter – Followers
- Google+ – Circlers
- YouTube – Subscribers

- Pinterest – Followers
- Snapchat - Friend
- Instagram - Followers

Audience: Metrics the people who chose to join the social media community for a particular brand. Each social channel has its own terminology:

Big Data: Commonly refers to situations with datasets so large that standard database management applications have a hard time processing. In the world of social-media, big data refers to the complex and inconsistent data structures that one brand must compile and measure against to tell their story.

Call To Action (CTA): an instruction to the audience to provoke an immediate response, usually using an imperative verb such as "click below to find out more" or "Like our page to join the movement."

Click-Through Rate: The number of clicks on a post divided by the number of impressions for the post.

ClickZ Live: Formally known as SES (Search Engine Strategies) Search Engine Strategies is a conference series focused on search engine marketing and search engine optimization.

CMO (Chief Marketing Officer): A corporate executive responsible for marketing activities in an organization.

Competitive Analysis: Competitive analysis and benchmarking allows brands to monitor and measure the effectiveness of their campaigns against the competition. This type of analysis provides valuable insights and gives context to how a brand's metrics relate to others in their specific market, or the greater social community.

Content Performance: Tracking and analyzing the success (or failure) of a piece of content. Understanding what causes certain content to succeed and others to fail gives brands better insight into where they should devote time and resources to reach their goals.

Crowdsourcing: Using a brand's audience to create new content.

Customer Service: (AKA Social Customer Service) The worlds of customer service and marketing are more interconnected as consumers expect responses to inquiries through "marketing" channels. To build a strong social community, brands must think about the customer service implications and incorporate CS goals into their strategy.

Day Parting: Measuring the effectiveness of an outbound message at different times of the day to understand what the optimum posting time and frequency is.

Demographics: Understanding the similarities and differences of an audience is a key component for crafting messages that resonate, and executing social campaigns that drive engagement.

Distribution of Comments: How comments relate to one another, across a variety of social channels.

Engagement as % of Audience: Adding up total engagement actions across all social networks and then dividing that by total audience.

Engagement Decay: The progressive decrease over time in engagement rate for a piece of content or collection of content.

Engagement per Fan/Follower: Adding up total engagement actions for one network and dividing by the number of fans (or followers) for that particular network.

Engagement Rate: Engagement activities on a particular social channel divided by the associated audience. This can be looked at holistically for an entire presence, for a specific channel, or for a specific post or activity type.

Facebook Engagement: Combination of all the activity on a brand's Fan Page: shares, PTAT, comments, clicks and likes. For more Facebook definitions, visit the Simply Measured 60+ Insights Definitions post.

Flacker: A term sometimes used to describe a publicist or press agent, to promote or publicize.

Geographic Distribution: Where in the world the audience is physically located.

GIF: Graphics Interchange Format. GIFs are image files that are compressed to reduce transfer time. The proper pronunciation of the acronym is a soft "g" sound: like JIF.

Google+ Engagement: Combination of all the activity on a brand's G+ page: Reshares, comments, and +1s.

Hot Button: A topic or issue that is highly charged emotionally or politically.

HTML (Hypertext Markup Language): A standardized system for tagging text files to achieve font, color, graphic, and hyperlink effects on World Wide Web pages.

Interactions: The way in which a brand responds to and builds relationships with their social audience.

JPEG (Joint Photographic Experts Group): A format for compressing image files.

Keyword Frequency: The number of times that a particular keyword or phrase is found within your social graph.

Keywords: A word or concept of great significance. In reference to PR, a word that is most likely used when searching a specific business, topic, or idea.

Klout Score/Influencers: Klout is a mechanism for measuring how influential a person or brand is on a particular social channel. It provides brands with a way of identifying existing influencers in their audience as well as identifying new ones.

KPI (Key Performance Indicator): While performance indicators can be measured by a variety of things, the main goal of utilizing them is to help businesses or organizations define and measure progress toward their goals.

Meta Description Tags: (As defined by Moz with commentary by Lisa Buyer.) Meta description tags, while not important to search engine rankings, are still important in gaining user click-through from SERPs, gaining media attention, and social media shares. These short paragraphs are a webmaster's (and public relations pro or blogger) opportunity to advertise content to searchers and to let them know exactly whether the given page contains the information they're looking for.

The meta description should include the keywords intelligently, but also create a compelling description that a searcher (like the media or your target audience) will want to click. Direct relevance to the page and uniqueness between each page's meta description is key. The description should optimally be between 150–160 characters.

Meta Title Tags: This is part of the data that is not visible on a website but is a sentence or headline used to describe the title of a web page or blog post. It should be well-written with keywords because it displayed in search engine results pages and will influence click-throughs (visits) to a website or blog. Title tags are also part of what makes people decide whether to visit your site when it shows up in the search results. The title tag should contain important keywords to help the search engine determine what the page is about.

Social PR Secret
"Write title tags for humans; format them for search engines."
via @schachin
This is good advice for public relations professionals to educate themselves on optimizing writing for best exposure in search and social.

People Talking About This (PTAT): The number of unique users who "create a story about you" on Facebook.

Pinterest Engagement: Combination of all the activity on a brand's Pinterest page: repins, comments, and likes.

Post Mix: The makeup of your outbound content types. Each channel has it's own terminology: Facebook - Posts; Twitter - Tweets; Google+ - Posts; YouTube – Uploads; Snapchat – Snaps; Instagram – Posts; and Pinterest - Pins.

Post Reach: The estimated number of individuals who see a piece of outbound content at least once during a specific period of time.

Potential Impressions: The number of times a piece of content could be displayed, regardless of whether or not it is interacted with, during a specific time period.

Potential Reach: The total potential number of individuals in a brand's audience that could have the opportunity to see a piece content during a specific period of time.

PPC (Pay Per Click): A business model where a company that has placed an advertisement on a website pays a sum of money to the host website when a user clicks on to the advertisement. Simply, "the amount spent to get an advertisement clicked."

PR (Public Relations): Practice of managing the spread of information between an individual or an organization and the public.

Presence: The complete collection of a brand's presence across all the social networks.

Pubcon: An annual search and social media marketing conference. Pubcon is short for "Pubconference" referencing its early years held in pubs around the world.

Reach: The total combined amount of a brand's audience, compounded by the friends of the audience and anyone in the greater community who is talking about or engaging with the brand.

Resonance: How a particular message triggers a reaction across the entire social graph, all the while creating valuable touchpoints that drive back to the original content location.

Response Rate: The percent of audience inquiries are responded to within a certain amount of time.

Response Time: How quickly a brand responds to engagement activities and inquiries from their audience.

ROI (Return on Investment): The most common profitability ratio.

ROSI (Return on Social Investment): Calculating this metric can be tricky. Taking known social media expenses and mapping that against revenue generated by social endeavors, will give an estimated ROSI. Calculating this metric at the campaign level gives brands perspective and understanding as to which campaigns are most effective for particular goals.

Sentiment Analysis: Detecting and understanding how the audience is reacting to a brand, either positively or negatively.

SEO (Search Engine Optimization): Strategies, tactics, and methods used to increase the number of visitors to a website by obtaining a high placement in a search results page of a search engine such as Google or Bing.

SERP (Search Engine Result Page): The results page that a search engine displays with the results of a search. An example of this would be if you type "Social PR Secrets" into Google, the SERP is the page of results that are displayed after you hit search.

Share of Audience: How does a brand's audience compare to their competition.

Share of Engagement: How does a brand's engagement metrics compare to their competition.

Share of Voice: How big a brand's slice of the conversation is compared to their competition.

SMO: Social Media Optimization

Social Listening & Monitoring: Social listening (aka monitoring) is the practice of identifying engagement opportunities and monitoring brand perceptions across all social channels, not just the ones a brand owns. Active listening and monitoring helps brands better understand what is going in the marketplace.

Topical Influencer: Who the influencers are on a particular subject.

Total Exposure Metrics & Social Graph: Total exposure is the size of a brand's primary audience combined with the greater community that a brand has the potential to reach and engage.

The social graph is the interconnected relationship between a brand, their audience, and the greater community. Understanding both of these elements helps brands realize their social media potential and puts context around where they fit in the greater social community.

True Reach: The actual number of individuals who see a piece of outbound content during a specific period of time.

Twitter Engagement: Combination of all the activity on a brand's Twitter account: ReTweets, mentions, hearts, replies, and clicks. Curious to learn more about your Twitter presence? Try the Simply Measured Free Twitter Follower Report!

Virality: The rate at which a brand's content spreads across the social graph. In some instances, the success of a piece of content is tied to how viral it becomes.

VSMM (Visual Social Media Marketing):

YouTube Engagement: Combination of all the activity on a brand's YouTube channel: comments, ratings, and shares.

Source:

Simply Measured (bit.ly/1uEkspG)

Made in the USA
Columbia, SC
19 September 2017